THE FUTURE OF HYDRAULIC FRACTURING ON FEDERALLY MANAGED LANDS

OVERSIGHT HEARING

BEFORE THE

SUBCOMMITTEE ON ENERGY AND MINERAL RESOURCES

OF THE

COMMITTEE ON NATURAL RESOURCES U.S. HOUSE OF REPRESENTATIVES

ONE HUNDRED FOURTEENTH CONGRESS

FIRST SESSION

Wednesday, July 15, 2015

Serial No. 114–15

Printed for the use of the Committee on Natural Resources

Available via the World Wide Web: http://www.fdsys.gov
or
Committee address: http://naturalresources.house.gov

U.S. GOVERNMENT PUBLISHING OFFICE

95–556 PDF   WASHINGTON : 2016

For sale by the Superintendent of Documents, U.S. Government Publishing Office
Internet: bookstore.gpo.gov   Phone: toll free (866) 512–1800; DC area (202) 512–1800
Fax: (202) 512–2104   Mail: Stop IDCC, Washington, DC 20402–0001

COMMITTEE ON NATURAL RESOURCES

ROB BISHOP, UT, *Chairman*
RAÚL M. GRIJALVA, AZ, *Ranking Democratic Member*

Don Young, AK
Louie Gohmert, TX
Doug Lamborn, CO
Robert J. Wittman, VA
John Fleming, LA
Tom McClintock, CA
Glenn Thompson, PA
Cynthia M. Lummis, WY
Dan Benishek, MI
Jeff Duncan, SC
Paul A. Gosar, AZ
Raúl R. Labrador, ID
Doug LaMalfa, CA
Jeff Denham, CA
Paul Cook, CA
Bruce Westerman, AR
Garret Graves, LA
Dan Newhouse, WA
Ryan K. Zinke, MT
Jody B. Hice, GA
Aumua Amata Coleman Radewagen, AS
Thomas MacArthur, NJ
Alexander X. Mooney, WV
Cresent Hardy, NV
Vacancy

Grace F. Napolitano, CA
Madeleine Z. Bordallo, GU
Jim Costa, CA
Gregorio Kilili Camacho Sablan, CNMI
Niki Tsongas, MA
Pedro R. Pierluisi, PR
Jared Huffman, CA
Raul Ruiz, CA
Alan S. Lowenthal, CA
Matt Cartwright, PA
Donald S. Beyer, Jr., VA
Norma J. Torres, CA
Debbie Dingell, MI
Ruben Gallego, AZ
Lois Capps, CA
Jared Polis, CO
Vacancy

Jason Knox, *Chief of Staff*
Lisa Pittman, *Chief Counsel*
David Watkins, *Democratic Staff Director*
Sarah Parker, *Democratic Deputy Chief Counsel*

————

SUBCOMMITTEE ON ENERGY AND MINERAL RESOURCES

DOUG LAMBORN, CO, *Chairman*
ALAN S. LOWENTHAL, CA, *Ranking Democratic Member*

Louie Gohmert, TX
Robert J. Wittman, VA
John Fleming, LA
Glenn Thompson, PA
Cynthia M. Lummis, WY
Dan Benishek, MI
Jeff Duncan, SC
Paul A. Gosar, AZ
Raúl R. Labrador, ID
Paul Cook, CA
Garret Graves, LA
Ryan K. Zinke, MT
Jody B. Hice, GA
Alexander X. Mooney, WV
Cresent Hardy, NV
Rob Bishop, UT, *ex officio*

Jim Costa, CA
Niki Tsongas, MA
Matt Cartwright, PA
Donald S. Beyer, Jr., VA
Ruben Gallego, AZ
Lois Capps, CA
Jared Polis, CO
Vacancy
Vacancy
Vacancy
Vacancy
Vacancy
Vacancy
Raúl M. Grijalva, AZ, *ex officio*

————

(II)

CONTENTS

OVERSIGHT HEARING ON THE FUTURE OF HYDRAULIC FRACTURING ON FEDERALLY MANAGED LANDS

Wednesday, July 15, 2015
U.S. House of Representatives
Subcommittee on Energy and Mineral Resources
Committee on Natural Resources
Washington, DC

The subcommittee met, pursuant to notice, at 10:43 a.m., in room 1324, Longworth House Office Building, Hon. Doug Lamborn [Chairman of the Subcommittee] presiding.

Present: Representatives Lamborn, Gohmert, Fleming, Lummis, Benishek, Gosar, Labrador, Cook, Zinke, Mooney, Hardy, Bishop; Lowenthal, Costa, Tsongas, Cartwright, Beyer, Gallego, Capps, Polis, and Grijalva.

Dr. FLEMING [presiding]. The Subcommittee on Energy and Mineral Resources will come to order. I am not Chairman Lamborn.

[Laughter.]

Dr. FLEMING. I am Fleming, but I am standing in for—or sitting in for Lamborn, for the moment. He is held up in another Committee activity.

The subcommittee is meeting today to hear testimony on the future of hydraulic fracturing on federally managed lands.

Under Committee Rule 4(f), any oral opening statements at hearings are limited to the Chairman and the Ranking Member, and the Vice Chairman and a designee of the Ranking Member. This will allow us to hear from our witnesses sooner, and help Members keep to their schedules. Therefore, I ask unanimous consent that all other Members' opening statements be made part of the hearing record, if they are submitted to the Subcommittee clerk by 5:00 p.m. today.

[No response.]

Dr. FLEMING. Hearing no objection, so ordered.

I now recognize myself for an opening statement.

STATEMENT OF THE HON. JOHN FLEMING, A REPRESENTATIVE IN CONGRESS FROM THE STATE OF LOUISIANA

Dr. FLEMING. For decades the states have been regulating hydraulic fracturing on Federal lands managed by the BLM without incident. And now, the BLM arrogantly seeks to second guess state regulations with a one-size-fits-all final rule on hydraulic fracturing.

This subcommittee has warned about the adverse effects the BLM's poorly planned hydraulic fracturing regulations would have on tribes and states with Federal lands, and now we have the words of a Federal judge echoing our warnings. He stated, and I

(1)

quote, "There is a showing of a credible threat of irreparable harm: in cost of compliance, as well as the loss of revenue," to the states and industry.

Now, why do states need to suffer this irreparable harm? The BLM tells us it is necessary because there are "concerns about whether fracturing can lead to or cause the contamination of underground water sources," and that only half of the states with oil and gas leases on the Federal lands have modern hydraulic fracturing regulations.

Well, let's look at the facts. When the final rule was released, the BLM acknowledged that 99.3 percent of all well completions on Federal or tribal land occurred in states with hydraulic fracturing regulations. What is more telling is how the BLM has never identified a single jurisdiction that lacks sufficient regulatory protections in which hydraulic fracturing occurs on Federal lands.

Furthermore, the EPA's recent study finding that there had been no "widespread, systemic impacts on drinking water resources in the United States," clearly demonstrates that states have been successful in regulating hydraulic fracturing and ensuring the protection of drinking water resources.

These facts highlight that states were proactive in regulating the process of hydraulic fracturing, and that they have been successful in doing so. I would say that the BLM's final rule on hydraulic fracturing is nothing more than a frivolous regulatory exercise, if not for the severe and unfortunate consequences the rule carries.

In an attempt to address concerns from states and tribes about possible duplicative efforts, the BLM established a variance provision. This subsection permits states or tribes to seek the application of their rules on Federal land if those rules "are demonstrated to be equal to or more protective" than the BLM's.

Let me be clear about what this variance provision is. It is merely a means by which the BLM may interpret state or tribal regulations on Federal lands. So when the final rule states, "variances may be granted to states and tribes," there is actually no grant. Neither the states nor the tribes receive any cognizable right or exercisable claim to continue implementing their hydraulic fracturing regulations on Federal lands, as has been the practice for decades.

As such, the variance provision only permits the BLM the opportunity to avoid its own regulations. How this redundant exercise will avoid duplicative efforts is beyond me. Inherently, it appears to encourage duplicative efforts, and will only lead to further confusion within the BLM state offices.

What is further troubling is the approach of the BLM toward those states who, in good faith, have attempted to obtain a variance. Like the rest of the rule, the BLM failed to provide any nationwide or baseline guidance that would have informed the state offices on how to proceed in the variance discussions. As such, not a single variance agreement has been entered into.

After examining the BLM's attempted roll out of this rule over the past few months, I must say, that if any group should be thrilled the judge postponed the effective date of the rule, it should be the BLM. Without this stay, the implementation of the rule would have been a national embarrassment, and would have effectively paused hydraulic fracturing on Federal and tribal lands for the foreseeable future.

Maybe if this had been an emergency rulemaking in which the BLM had a limited time frame to address a severe issue, these major oversights and lack of preparedness would be excusable. However, that is not the case. It is simply inexcusable that after 3 years, numerous stakeholder meetings, and over a million comments, that BLM can't even provide standardized guidance to its state offices.

Unfortunately, it is too late for the BLM to withdraw this rule. And so, the Nation is left with an uncertain future for hydraulic fracturing on Federal lands.

These are Mr. Lamborn's words, but I agree with every single one of them.

[The prepared statement of Mr. Lamborn follows:]

PREPARED STATEMENT OF THE HON. DOUG LAMBORN, CHAIRMAN, SUBCOMMITTEE ON ENERGY AND MINERAL RESOURCES

For decades, the states have been regulating hydraulic fracturing on Federal lands managed by the BLM without incident. And now, the BLM arrogantly seeks to second guess state regulations with a one-size-fits-all final rule on hydraulic fracturing.

This subcommittee has warned about the adverse effects the BLM's poorly planned hydraulic fracturing regulations would have on tribes and states with Federal lands. And now, we have the words of a Federal judge echoing our warnings. He stated, and I quote, "there is a showing of a credible threat of irreparable harm: [in] cost of compliance, as well as the loss of revenue," to the states and industry.

Now, why do the states need to suffer this irreparable harm? The BLM tells us it is necessary because there are "concerns about whether [hydraulic] fracturing can lead to or cause the contamination of underground water sources," and that only half of the states with oil and gas leases on Federal lands have modern hydraulic fracturing regulations.

Well, let's look at the facts. When the final rule was released, the BLM acknowledged that 99.3 percent of all well completions on Federal or tribal land occurred in states with hydraulic fracturing regulations. What is more telling, is how the BLM has *never* identified a single jurisdiction that lacks sufficient regulatory protections in which hydraulic fracturing occurs on Federal lands.

Furthermore, the EPA's recent study finding that there had been no "widespread, systemic impacts on drinking water resources in the United States," clearly demonstrates that states have been successful in regulating hydraulic fracturing and ensuring the protection of drinking water resources.

These facts highlight that states were proactive in regulating the process of hydraulic fracturing, and that they have been successful in doing so. I would say that the BLM's final rule on hydraulic fracturing is nothing more than a frivolous regulatory exercise, if not for the severe and unfortunate consequences the rule carries.

In an attempt to "address concerns from states and tribes about possible duplicative efforts," the BLM established a variance provision. This subsection permits states or tribes to seek the application of their rules on Federal land if those rules "are demonstrated to be equal to or more protective" than the BLM's.

Let me be clear about what this variance provision is: it is merely a means by which the BLM may interpret state or tribal regulations on Federal lands. So when the final rule states, "variances may be granted to states and tribes"—there is actually no grant. Neither the states, nor the tribes receive any cognizable right or exercisable claim to continue implementing their hydraulic fracturing regulations on Federal lands, as has been the practice for decades.

As such, the "variance provision" *only* permits the BLM the opportunity to avoid its own regulations. How this redundant exercise will avoid duplicative efforts is beyond me. Inherently, it appears to encourage duplicative efforts, and will only lead to further confusion within the BLM state offices.

What is further troubling is the approach of the BLM toward those states who in good faith have attempted to obtain a variance. Like the rest of the rule, the BLM failed to provide any nationwide, or baseline guidance that would have informed the state offices on how to proceed in the variance discussions. As such, *not a single* variance agreement has been entered into.

After examining the BLM's attempted roll out of this rule over the past few months, I must say, that if any group should be thrilled the judge postponed the effective date of the rule, it should be the BLM. Without this stay, the implementation of the rule would have been a national embarrassment, and would have effectively paused hydraulic fracturing on Federal and tribal lands for the foreseeable future.

Maybe if this had been an emergency rulemaking in which the BLM had a limited time frame to address a severe issue, these major oversights and lack of preparedness would be excusable. However, that is not the case. It is simply inexcusable that after 3 years, numerous stakeholder meetings, and over a million comments, the BLM can't even provide standardized guidance to its state offices.

Unfortunately, it is too late for the BLM to withdraw this rule—and so, the Nation is left with an uncertain future for hydraulic fracturing on Federal lands.

————

Dr. FLEMING. With that, I will yield to the Ranking Member for his opening remarks.

STATEMENT OF THE HON. ALAN S. LOWENTHAL, A REP-RESENTATIVE IN CONGRESS FROM THE STATE OF CALIFORNIA

Mr. LOWENTHAL. Thank you, Chairman Fleming, and thank you to the witnesses for being here, particularly Director Kornze, who has faced a considerable amount of grilling from both sides of the aisle over this rule in the past few months. And each time you have defended it and your agency in a forthright and highly commendable manner. Mr. Director, it is good to see you again.

I have heard a lot of complaints from the oil and gas industry and my colleagues on the other side of the aisle about what they see as overblown concerns about fracking. To them, fracking is perfectly safe, and anyone who questions that is needlessly scaring people. But when it comes to overblown hysteria, nothing matches the industry's reaction to the Bureau of Land Management's fracking rule.

If you listen to them, you would think that this rule was a royal edict, completely changing the rules of the game on Federal lands, and that the BLM has never regulated oil and gas before. But you would be wrong. Because this rule is nothing but a modest modernization of long-standing BLM regulations to take into account how the industry currently operates.

One point there appears to be a lot of confusion over is how this rule would affect the states. Let me make this clear. And this is not my opinion. On Federal lands, the BLM sets the floor. Let me say that again: On Federal lands, the BLM sets the floor. The states are free to put the ceiling wherever they want. And, yes, even on Federal lands, companies must meet those state standards. That is how things worked yesterday, that is how they work today, and that is how they will work the day after the fracking rule takes effect.

Forget about the state's variance provision. I am not talking about that, because it is really unnecessary. States will be able to set their rules, and companies on Federal lands will have to follow them, variance or no variance.

I am sorry that Mr. Fitzsimmons is not here from Wyoming, because it is great that Wyoming has strong fracking regulations. I am pleased to hear that. Wyoming would be free to enforce these regulations when this rule goes into effect, just as they are right now, because of their stronger drilling regulations. But let's also be clear that not all states have regulations as good as Wyoming's. And when it comes to protecting public lands and public resources in all 50 states, we have given the BLM a statutory mandate, and it would be irresponsible, if not illegal, for them to simply ignore that.

And that authority goes way back. It may surprise people to know that regulations covering all forms of well stimulation, including fracking, were first issued in 1942, even though fracking barely existed at the time. Those were issued by the U.S. Geological Survey, who was in charge of this issue before the BLM.

Those regulations were in place when the Safe Drinking Water Act was passed in 1974, and the House report on the Safe Drinking Water Act says very clearly, and I quote, "The committee does not intend any of the provisions of this bill to repeal or to limit any authority that the USGS may have under other legislation." That is about as clear-cut and dry as you can get.

Now times have changed, and these regulations were last updated in the 1980s to exempt routine fracturing jobs. But times changed again, and now fracking is significantly different than it was 30 years ago. It is long past time for the BLM to modernize these out-of-date regulations and to provide to the industry and to the states proper baseline protections for public lands from coast to coast.

Now, I would like to say that despite my bewilderment at the complaints from the industry and the states, I am also very sympathetic to the concerns of our tribes. As we saw from a Government Accountability Office report last month, there are serious problems with the way that energy development on tribal lands is managed, problems that go back for decades.

While we have to consider carefully this rule's impact on the tribes, their overall concern with energy development is real—they are real, they are serious, and they deserve a more thorough investigation by this committee.

But for companies operating on public lands, this rule is nothing more than a small step to bring BLM's outdated regulations, which they have operated under for decades, into the 21st century.

Thank you, Mr. Chair, and I yield back.

[The prepared statement of Mr. Lowenthal follows:]

PREPARED STATEMENT OF THE HON. ALAN S. LOWENTHAL, RANKING MEMBER, SUBCOMMITTEE ON ENERGY AND MINERAL RESOURCES

Thank you Mr. Chairman, and thank you to the witnesses for being here, particularly Director Kornze, who has faced a considerable amount of grilling from both sides of the aisle over this rule in the past few months, and each time he has defended it and his agency in a forthright and highly commendable manner. Mr. Director, it is good to see you again.

I have heard a lot of complaints from the oil and gas industry and my colleagues on the other side about what they see as overblown concerns about fracking. To them, fracking is perfectly safe, and anyone who questions that is needlessly scaring people.

But when it comes to real overblown hysteria, nothing matches the industry's reaction to the Bureau of Land Management's fracking rule. If you listened to them, you would think this rule was a royal edict completely changing the rules of the game on Federal lands, and that the BLM has never regulated oil and gas before.

But you would be wrong. Because this rule is nothing but a modest modernization of long-standing BLM regulations to take into account how the industry currently operates.

One point that there appears to be a lot of confusion over is how this rule would affect states. Let me make this clear. And this is not my opinion, this is fact: this rule does not affect a state's ability to set its own regulations. On *Federal lands*, BLM sets *the floor*. The states are free to put the ceiling wherever they want. And, yes, *even on Federal lands* companies must meet those state standards.

That's how things worked yesterday, that's how they work today, and that's how they will work on the day the fracking rule takes effect.

Forget about the state variance provision. I'm not talking about that. Because it's unnecessary. States will be able to set their rules, and companies on Federal lands will have to follow them, variance or no variance.

I think it's great that Wyoming has strong fracking regulations. I'm pleased to hear that. You would be free to enforce those regulations just as you are *right now* for your stronger drilling regulations.

But not all states have regulations as good as Wyoming's. And when it comes to protecting public land and public resources in all 50 states, we have given the BLM a statutory mandate, and it would be irresponsible, if not illegal, for them simply to ignore that.

And that authority goes back quite a way. It may surprise people to know that regulations covering *all forms* of well stimulation, *including fracking*, were issued in 1942, even though fracking barely existed at the time. Those were issued by the U.S. Geological Survey, who was in charge of this issue before the BLM.

Those regulations were in place when the Safe Drinking Water Act was passed in 1974. And the House report on the Safe Drinking Water Act says very clearly, "The committee does not intend any of the provisions of this bill to repeal or limit any authority the USGS may have under any other legislation."

That is about as cut and dry as you can get.

Now, times changed, and those regulations were updated in the 1980s to exempt routine fracturing jobs. But times changed again, and now fracking is significantly different than it was 30 years ago. It is long past time for BLM to modernize these out-of-date regulations and provide proper *baseline protections* for public lands from coast to coast.

Now, I would like to say that despite my bewilderment at the complaints from the industry and the states, I am very sympathetic to the concerns of our tribes. As we saw from a Government Accountability Office report last month, there are serious problems with the way that energy development on tribal lands is managed, problems that go back decades.

While we have to consider carefully this rule's impacts on the tribes, their overall concerns with energy development are real, they are serious, and they deserve a more thorough investigation by this committee.

But for companies operating on public lands, this rule is nothing more than a small step to bring BLM's outdated regulations, which they have operated under for decades, toward the 21st century.

Thank you, Mr. Chairman, and I yield back.

————

Dr. FLEMING. The gentleman yields. The Chair now recognizes Mr. Grijalva for an opening statement.

STATEMENT OF THE HON. RAÚL M. GRIJALVA, A REPRESENT-ATIVE IN CONGRESS FROM THE STATE OF ARIZONA

Mr. GRIJALVA. Thank you very much, Mr. Chairman, for your courtesy, and also the Ranking Member, as well. Of course, thanking the witnesses for being here, and the Director, for his professionalism and on occasion his endurance, as well. As the Ranking Member indicated, criticism has come from all sides of the committee regarding the rule, and through that all, your professionalism is very much appreciated. Thank you.

As I said before, I believe that the Bureau of Land Management's rule for fracking is much too weak. I am pleased to discover that several western states completely agree with me. Throughout their court arguments, the states point out that they have much stronger regulations than BLM, which means that companies in those states can keep going on with their business as usual, regardless of risks they might be posing to our air, to our water, to our health, and to the economic equity of homeowners throughout many of those lands.

That is a problem. The Federal Government should be raising the bar, not settling for the lowest common denominator. The rule is necessary, and will have some benefits, particularly in states that don't have robust rules. But we should be doing more. Yet for some reason, the states and industry are not thanking BLM for issuing a rule that will have very little impact in the field, and cost almost nothing. They aren't thanking Congress for leaving in place the loopholes that exempt them from a number of our fundamental environmental laws. No. Instead, they are complaining that the rule is too confusing, too redundant, too expensive.

This has to be a reflex. If a regulation comes out, it must be bad, so they have to challenge it. Never mind that the rule allows states to continue to regulate as they wish. Never mind that it actually simplifies requirements for companies in some cases. Never mind that the BLM has been very accommodating and bending over backwards to try to meet the concerns of the states and industry.

The industry creates confusion. It invents unrealistic costs. Then their allies on the Hill rush to their defense. This rule does not do as much as it should, but it also doesn't do half of what the Republicans claim. The rule does not do as much as I would like it to, but it is much better than nothing. And that is what the Majority would precisely have us do: nothing. Nothing keeps our land, our water, our air, and our health at risk, and that would be irresponsible.

I appreciate the time, and I yield back.

Dr. FLEMING. The gentleman yields back, so I think we are ready for our testimony to begin.

Before I begin with the witness introductions, I would like to mention that one of today's witnesses, Mr. Tom Fitzsimmons of the Wyoming Oil and Gas Conservation Commission, was not able to join us here today, due to weather-related travel issues. Though he is not able to testify, he will still be able to answer any questions submitted for the record.

I also would like to enter his testimony into the hearing record.
[No response.]

Dr. FLEMING. And, hearing no objection, so ordered.
[The prepared statement of Mr. Fitzsimmons follows:]

PREPARED STATEMENT OF TOM FITZSIMMONS, PE, COMMISSIONER, WYOMING OIL AND GAS CONSERVATION COMMISSION, CODY, WYOMING

Chairman Lamborn, Ranking Member Lowenthal and members of the committee, thank you for the opportunity to appear before you today.

I serve as a commissioner on the Wyoming Oil and Gas Conservation Commission as well as chairman of the Wyoming Enhanced Oil Recovery Commission. When not serving in these roles, I provide expert witness testimony in business and technical matters concerning the oil and gas industry. Prior to my involvement in the state commissions, I was actively involved in fracturing several hundreds of oil and gas wells as a producer and service provider. I have over 32 years in the oil and gas industry in Wyoming, Montana, and across the West.

The state of Wyoming, through the Wyoming Oil and Gas Conservation Commission (hereinafter WOGCC), has in place a comprehensive and time-tested hydraulic fracturing regulatory program. Implemented in 2010, Wyoming's Hydraulic Fracturing rule has been modeled by other state regulatory agencies and has been referred to by the Secretary of the Interior as a "standard" for other states to follow. The Bureau of Land Management (BLM) hydraulic fracturing rule that was set to become effective last month is unnecessary and is a threat to our state's economy.

STATE AGENCIES ARE BEST SUITED TO MANAGE HYDRAULIC FRACTURING

Successful regulatory oversight hinges upon a focused approach. As mentioned, Wyoming's rule on hydraulic fracturing is comprehensive. From the rule's inception, it was designed to be robust. It requires disclosure and covers many aspects of well stimulation including, but not limited to, groundwater protection through downhole design and testing and baseline groundwater testing for chemical additives. In addition, the WOGCC governs the recovery of resources so that oil and gas is optimally developed with the guiding principle and legislative mandate to avoid waste.

Wyoming's cohesive team of industry experts reside in a single office overseen by the Commissioners, located in the center of Wyoming. The team, led by Oil and Gas Supervisor Mark Watson, is experienced and efficient. The Wyoming team understands the regional oil and gas potential made possible through technologies such as enhanced oil recovery while balancing the needs of the environment and responsible development. In contrast, the BLM has 10 field offices located across many miles in Wyoming—each staffed to serve a wide variety of needs—but not focused to regulate hydraulic fracturing. This is not a condemnation of BLM staff, but rather an insight of the value in allowing the states to apply a focused, local approach to regulation as opposed to a disjointed Federal agency lead by Washington, DC that promotes a "one-size-fits-all approach."

BLM's draft resource management plan for the Big Horn Basin contained, in my opinion, two critical flaws when it was released. The flaws were: (1) the pipeline corridor infrastructure was not tied to adjoining basin pipeline corridors; and (2) the BLM failed to recognize almost 2.0 billion barrels of reserve potential through enhanced oil recovery. These flaws were errors of omission due to lack of focus, time and industry expertise in the agency at every level.

The lack of focus and expertise within the BLM results in long delays in the permitting process. Although the cost of permitting for a Federal APD is 190 times higher than the cost of a state permit, it still takes two to five times longer to approve a Federal APD. With the addition of the BLM's Hydraulic Fracturing rule, we can only expect permitting delays to increase even more. Further, the lack of regulatory focus has many operators shifting their investment to fee and state managed minerals. As mentioned above the legislative mandate of the WOGCC is to minimize waste. Sparse development on Federal minerals will result in waste. Promoting waste through developing more unnecessary bureaucratic "red tape" through unnecessary rules is not the way to best develop America's abundance of oil and natural gas or maximize revenue for the Federal Government for the benefit of all American citizens.

CONFUSION IN REGULATORY AUTHORITY RESULTS IN AVOIDANCE OF MINERAL DEVELOPMENT

Michael Madrid (BLM Deputy State Director for Minerals) testified before the Legislature's Select Committee on Federal Natural Resource Management on July 9, 2015 in Cheyenne, Wyoming. Mr. Madrid conceded that it would be very difficult to manage Hydraulic Fracturing rules by two agencies on the same well. We should listen to the people who are on the front line of this issue. Overlapping rules complicates development when the permitting and the reporting process are doubled. Other challenges that create confusion include:

The possibility exists for the BLM to disapprove a hydraulic fracture stimulation already approved by the WOGCC simply because portions of the Wyoming approved procedure may differ from the BLM rule even though certain portions of the Wyoming rule exceeded BLM requirements.

When it comes to chemical disclosure and trademark protection, Wyoming has a well thought-out approach that allows service companies to prequalify their trade secret products before being used on a fracture treatment. Wyoming's single application process is efficient for both the state and the industry. In contrast, the BLM process presents a risk to service companies that their proprietary information may be compromised if the trade secret status is rejected after the fact, leaving no recourse other than litigation to protect proprietary information.

Further, the BLM rules will require that the operator submit a new and complete trade secret request for each hydraulic-fracture-treatment, in which a trade secret protected product is used, even if they have previously submitted numerous trade secret requests for that same product. This requirement places an unnecessary data management burden on all involved with no additional benefit. The objective of this requirement could be managed more efficiently. All of this uncertainty results in fewer companies willing to risk their investment on development of Federal minerals. The economic impacts to the state of Wyoming and its cities, towns, and counties will be profoundly negative and can be avoided.

PREVENTION OF WASTE IS VITAL

The Wyoming Oil and Gas Conservation Commission is well known for its transparency of lease, production and well data presented on an easy to use Web platform. This platform allows oil and gas operators to evaluate other offset wells and thus improve their practices. For example, this transparency enables an engineer to learn from competitors and improve well performance which results in higher ultimate recovery from future wells. The BLM's hydraulic fracturing rule fails to consider the need for combining fracture treatment data with production performance. This oversight will make it nearly impossible to analyze the large volumes of data associated with production and well construction.

HF REGULATION SHOULD BE AT STATE LEVEL

For all these reasons, the members of the Wyoming Oil and Gas Conservation Commission believe it has effective hydraulic fracturing regulations in place that are carried out by highly skilled professionals who solely focus on these important matters as public servants. Wyoming's state regulations aim to protect our environment, maximize recovery of resources and promote responsible development. In addition, our baseline water testing requirements and chemical additive disclosure regulations help ensure public safety. The BLM rule is unnecessary, lacks focus, and fails to adequately promote responsible development. Wyoming has been a leader in the regulation of Hydraulic Fracturing. Wyoming's state rules were developed by industry, government, conservationists as well as other stakeholders working side by side to find the right balance. It is critical that the Federal Government defers jurisdiction to states with rules similar to Wyoming's to ensure timely development with reduced waste and confusion.

Thank you for the opportunity to appear before you today and I look forward to your questions.

————

Dr. FLEMING. Testifying today we have Mr. Neil Kornze, Director, Bureau of Land Management, U.S. Department of the Interior; Mr. Mike Olguin, Council Member, Southern Ute Indian Tribe; Mr. Lloyd Hetrick, Operations Engineering Advisor, Newfield Exploration Company; and Ms. Hannah Wiseman, Attorneys' Title Professor of Florida State University College of Law.

Let me remind the witnesses that, under our Committee Rules, they must limit their oral statements to 5 minutes. But the entire statement will appear in the record.

We work on a light system here. You have 5 minutes. You will be under a green light for the first 4 minutes, then yellow. When it turns red, if you haven't finished, go ahead and finish. Trust me, your entire testimony, as written, will appear in the record.

The Chair now recognizes Director Kornze to testify for 5 minutes.

STATEMENT OF NEIL KORNZE, DIRECTOR, BUREAU OF LAND MANAGEMENT, U.S. DEPARTMENT OF THE INTERIOR, WASHINGTON, DC

Mr. KORNZE. Thank you, Mr. Chairman, Ranking Member, members of the committee. It is great to be here with you today.

The BLM manages roughly 10 percent of the Nation's surface, and nearly a third of its minerals and soils. We manage these lands on behalf of the American people, under the framework of multiple use and sustained yield. Today the Bureau's work is more complex than ever, but we work very hard to make sure that the public's voice is heard in the actions that we take.

The BLM works diligently to fulfill its role in America's energy economy, by supporting the responsible development of oil and gas resources on public and Indian lands. During this Administration, oil production from those lands has increased 81 percent, tracking or exceeding comparable statewide trends. Some may contend that production on BLM-managed lands has not kept pace with national trends; the numbers, however, tell a very different story.

And, even though we oversee more than 100,000 wells across the country, we continue to make lands available for leasing far in excess of industry demand. Right now, industry holds 34 million acres of land for oil and gas development, but is only producing on a third of that. It is worth noting that last year the BLM made nearly 6 million acres of land available, but industry bid on only about 20 percent of that acreage.

It is also important to highlight that the BLM has issued roughly 6,000 drilling permits that are available, approved, and ready to go today, that are not being used by industry. This represents about 2 years' worth of work by the oil and gas industry on public and Indian lands, and we would like to see these permits put to work creating American energy and American jobs.

In supporting this development, our oil and gas program's highest priority is ensuring that the operations that it authorizes are safe and environmentally responsible. The hydraulic fracturing rule is critical to meeting that responsibility, because it establishes standards that are essential to protecting our shared environment, while also facilitating robust development.

Of the wells currently being drilled that BLM oversees, over 90 percent employ modern hydraulic fracturing techniques that are significantly more complex than those used in the near past. They are often much deeper, and also often coupled with horizontal drilling techniques. While these technological advances and the tremendous increase in their use has facilitated greater access to oil and gas, it has also necessitated that the BLM revisit its rules on hydraulic fracturing, which were last updated roughly 30 years ago.

The BLM's rule builds upon the existing regulatory framework and establishes reasonable common-sense baseline standards, as has been discussed here. It requires operators to construct sound wells, to disclose the chemicals they use, and to safely recover and handle waste fluids. Our rule was informed by our engineers, technical expertise, as well as that of state and tribal regulators, industry, and many other experts.

The BLM has a long history of regulating oil and gas activities on public lands, as you know. It also has an established track record of working closely with operators, tribes, and states to avoid duplication and delay. The ultimate implementation of the hydraulic fracturing rule will be no different.

We have been actively working with states and tribes that have hydraulic fracturing standards to evaluate the potential for variances. Unfortunately, those discussions had to be temporarily put on hold in response to the Wyoming District Court's order. We intend to continue this important work, once the litigation has been addressed.

Now, before closing, I would like to briefly mention the two pending legal challenges against the BLM's hydraulic fracturing rule. While I am very confident that the rule is consistent with the BLM statutory authorities, because of where we are in the process of defending our rule, the ongoing litigation could impact much of our discussion here today.

I am happy to discuss the requirements of the rule. However, in light of the litigation, there will likely be areas of inquiry that I won't be at liberty to explore in today's hearing. For example, I will be quite limited in what I can say regarding potential positive or negative impacts of the rule, or regarding arguments related to the BLM's authority to issue and enforce the rule. I appreciate your understanding on this point. I have been here twice in front of the House Natural Resources Committee to discuss this rule, and know that I share your desire to have a robust conversation on these issues.

Thank you for the opportunity to be with you today; I look forward to your questions.

[The prepared statement of Mr. Kornze follows:]

PREPARED STATEMENT OF NEIL KORNZE, DIRECTOR, BUREAU OF LAND MANAGEMENT, U.S. DEPARTMENT OF THE INTERIOR

Chairman Lamborn, Ranking Member Lowenthal, and members of the subcommittee, thank you for the opportunity to discuss the Bureau of Land Management's (BLM) final hydraulic fracturing regulations and their application to Federal, tribal, and Indian trust mineral resources. The BLM oil and gas program's highest priority is ensuring that the operations it authorizes on public and tribal lands are safe and environmentally responsible. This rule is critical to meeting that responsibility as we continue to offer millions of acres of public land for minerals development each year.

The BLM's rule establishes a consistent set of requirements designed to prevent problems in these complex hydraulic fracturing operations before they occur. It also will provide as much information as possible to the public about these operations that affect their public lands. The goals of the rule—safe and environmentally responsible operation and resource protection—are goals that we know the BLM shares with industry, states, tribes, and the American public. The expertise brought to these issues by those who participated in the rulemaking process was essential to producing a rule that will achieve these goals, and we are very appreciative of the time and skill invested by all concerned.

BACKGROUND

The BLM is responsible for protecting the resources and managing the uses of our Nation's public lands, which are located primarily in 12 western states, including Alaska. The BLM administers more land—over 245 million surface acres—than any other Federal agency. The BLM also manages approximately 700 million acres of onshore Federal mineral estate throughout the Nation, including the subsurface estate overlain by properties managed by other Federal agencies such as the Department of Defense and the U.S. Forest Service. In addition, the BLM, together with the Bureau of Indian Affairs (BIA), provides permitting and oversight services under the Indian Mineral Leasing Act of 1938 to approximately 56 million acres of land held in trust by the Federal Government on behalf of tribes and individual Indian owners. The BLM works closely with surface management agencies, including the BIA and tribal governments, in the management of these subsurface resources. We are also mindful of our agency's responsibility for stewardship of public land resources and Indian trust assets that generate substantial revenue for the U.S. Treasury, the states, tribal governments, and individual Indian owners.

In support of President Obama's balanced approach to energy, the BLM is committed to promoting safe, responsible, and environmentally sustainable domestic oil and gas production in a manner that will protect consumers, human health, and the environment, and reduce our dependence on foreign oil.

In Fiscal Year (FY) 2014, onshore Federal oil and gas royalties exceeded $3 billion, approximately half of which were paid directly to the states in which the development occurred. In Fiscal Year 2014, tribal oil and gas royalties exceeded $1 billion with all of those revenues paid to the tribes or individual Indian owners of the land on which the development occurred.

The BLM works diligently to fulfill its role in securing America's energy future, coordinating closely with partners across the country to ensure that development of oil and gas resources occurs in the right places and that those projects are managed safely and responsibly. In recent years, the BLM has overseen a significant increase in oil production from public lands, while also supporting continued natural gas production. Oil production from Federal and Indian lands in 2014 rose 12 percent from the previous year and is now up 81 percent since 2008—113 million barrels per year in 2008 to 205 million barrels per year in 2014. For comparison, nationwide oil production over the same period increased 73 percent. The BLM continues to make public lands available for oil and gas development in excess of industry demand. Additionally, today the BLM has responsibility for more than 100,000 existing oil and gas wells.

HYDRAULIC FRACTURING TECHNOLOGY

Hydraulic fracturing involves the injection of fluid under high pressure to create or enlarge fractures in the rocks containing oil and gas so that the fluids can flow more freely into the wellbore and thus increase production. The number of wells on BLM-managed public lands and on Indian lands that are stimulated by hydraulic fracturing techniques has increased steadily in recent years. Of wells currently being drilled, over 90 percent use modern hydraulic fracturing techniques for well completion.

These new well completions are typically significantly more complex than the wells drilled in the past. Modern hydraulic fracturing operations are often considerably deeper and coupled with relatively new horizontal drilling techniques to create greater wellbore volume in the reservoir, unlike those that occurred in the past which were used on a relatively small scale, to complete or to re-complete wells. The increasingly common combination of long lateral wellbores with the types of hydraulic fracturing used today has facilitated larger-scale operations that allow greater access to oil and gas resources in shale, tight gas, coalbed methane and conventional reservoirs across the country, sometimes in areas that have not previously or only recently experienced significant oil and gas development.

HYDRAULIC FRACTURING RULEMAKING CONSIDERATIONS

The Mineral Leasing Act of 1920 (MLA), as amended, directs the Secretary of the Interior to lease Federal oil and gas resources, and authorizes her to regulate the resulting oil and gas operations on those leases. The BLM has used this authority to develop regulations governing all aspects of oil and gas operations, including requirements related to surface-disturbing activities, production measurement, and well construction. The Indian Mineral Leasing Act extends this regulatory authority and the resultant rules to Indian oil and gas leases on trust lands (except those lands specifically excluded by statute). Finally, the Federal Land Policy and Management Act of 1976 (FLPMA) directs the BLM to manage the public lands using the principles of multiple use and sustained yield and to take any action necessary to prevent unnecessary or undue degradation. In fulfilling these objectives, FLPMA requires the BLM to manage public lands in a manner that protects the quality of their resources, including ecological, environmental, and water resources. On net, this statutory regime requires the BLM to balance responsible development with protection of the environment and public safety. The BLM works hard to ensure the appropriate balance is struck and that the applicable regulations and requirements are applied and enforced fairly and consistently across all the lands where the BLM has oversight responsibilities.

Prior to the issuance of the hydraulic fracturing rule, the BLM rules applicable to hydraulic fracturing were last updated over 30 years ago, and had not kept pace with the significant technological advances in hydraulic fracturing techniques and the tremendous increase in its use. The new rule is the culmination of 4 years of work by the BLM that began in November 2010 when it held its first public forum on this topic. Since that time, the BLM has published two proposed rules and held numerous meetings with the public and state officials, as well as many tribal consultations and meetings. The public comment period was open for a cumulative period of more than 210 days, during which time the BLM received and analyzed comments from more than 1.5 million individuals and groups. During this period, the BLM also studied state and tribal regulations, and consulted with state and tribal agencies, industry, and the public, including communities affected by oil and gas operations.

HYDRAULIC FRACTURING RULE REQUIREMENTS

Informed by the experience of its experts and the technical expertise and concerns of state regulators, tribes, industry, and the public, the BLM's hydraulic fracturing rule strengthens its existing oversight procedures and provides all stakeholders with additional assurance that operations are being carried out safely and responsibly.

Key components of the rule include provisions for ensuring the protection of groundwater supplies through requirements related to wellbore integrity. These include the placement of competent cement barriers between the wellbore and any potentially usable water zones through which the wellbore passes, which protects groundwater both from hydraulic fracturing fluids during drilling and from hydrocarbon contamination during production. The rule requires the interim storage of recovered waste fluids from the hydraulic fracturing operation in tanks, unless, under certain restrictive circumstances, specific approval for the use of pits has been granted to the operator, in order to minimize the potential for produced water spills that puts soil, water, and wildlife at risk. Additional measures requiring companies to submit more detailed information on the geology, depth, and location of pre-existing wells prior to drilling will lower the risk of cross-well contamination, which has become more prevalent as the use of horizontal drilling has significantly increased. To increase transparency, as much of this information as possible will be made available to the public. Finally, the rule requires companies to publicly disclose information about the chemicals used in their hydraulic fracturing processes on public lands within 30 days of completing the operations, subject to exceptions for information demonstrated to be a trade secret. Any information claimed to be a trade secret can be obtained by BLM for review of that claim.

These requirements were developed based on BLM's experience and technical expertise and work done by states, tribal authorities, and industry. During the 4 years the BLM spent preparing the rule, it benefited from the expertise of state and tribal regulators, and many provisions of the final rule reflect existing state standards. None of these requirements impose undue delays, costs, or procedures on operators.

WORK WITH STATES AND TRIBES

The BLM has established and maintained regulations governing oil and gas operations on public lands for decades, and has worked successfully with operators, tribes and state governments to avoid duplication and delay in the enforcement and monitoring of these regulations. The ultimate implementation of the hydraulic fracturing rule will continue this long-standing practice while also ensuring the BLM satisfies its obligations to ensure Federal standards are met. As explained above, the rule builds upon and updates the BLM's existing regulations to address an evolving technology, in order to provide consistent parameters for the conduct of hydraulic fracturing operations on BLM-managed public lands nationwide and Indian trust lands.

Of the 32 states with the potential for oil and gas development on federally managed mineral resources, slightly more than half have rules in place that address hydraulic fracturing, and those rules vary widely from state to state. Recognizing the expertise and experience that state and tribal authorities possess and consistent with its standard practice of ensuring the efficient implementation of its rules, the BLM had been working with states and tribes that have standards in place for hydraulic fracturing that meet or exceed those set by the BLM's rule to establish variances from those aspects of the BLM rule. That work has temporarily paused as a result of the litigation explained below. Following BLM approval of a variance, the BLM will enforce the specific state or tribal standard as part of its hydraulic fracturing regulatory program. In addition, the BLM will continue its coordination with states and tribes to establish or review and strengthen existing agreements related to oil and gas regulation and operations.

The BLM's overall intent for these coordination efforts is to minimize duplication and maximize efficiency, while also ensuring the applicable Federal standards are met. As this rule is implemented, the BLM will continuously work with states, tribes, and operators to maximize coordination and efficiency.

IMPLEMENTING THE RULE

The rule is expected to cost industry about $11,400 per hydraulic fracturing operation on average, which equates to no more than one-quarter of 1 percent of the cost of drilling a well. This is a modest cost considering the typical hydraulically fractured well costs between $5–$10 million to develop, the public interest in ensuring that these operations are conducted in an environmentally sound and safe manner, and in light of the high cost of remediating contaminated aquifers. The BLM is aware that industry, states, tribes, and the public share the same goal of safeguarding local communities, water quality, wildlife, and other resources from potential harm. For this reason, the BLM rule not only incorporates requirements from existing state and tribal rules, but industry best practices as well. In many cases, operators have voluntarily undertaken the best practices reflected in the BLM's rule. The rule ensures that those practices are maintained and adopted by all. As a result, the rule achieves a cost-effective path toward consistent permitting requirements and disclosure protocols for hydraulic fracturing operations.

The BLM has been taking a number of steps both internally and externally to prepare for the implementation of the rule in advance of its scheduled effective date. Internally, recognizing the central role wellbore integrity plays in maintaining safe operations, the BLM partnered with the Society of Petroleum Engineers to add more technical training for the BLM's engineers that emphasizes cementing and other critical aspects of hydraulic fracturing operations. The BLM will continue to offer, develop, and refine these technical training modules.

Externally, the BLM has undertaken outreach efforts to states, operators, trade associations, and other interested stakeholders. The BLM state offices have been meeting with their state counterparts, undertaking state-by-state comparisons of regulatory requirements in order to identify opportunities for variances, and to establish Memorandums of Understanding (MOUs) that will realize efficiencies and allow for successful implementation of the rule. To date, the BLM has had discussions with: the North Dakota Industrial Commission; the Wyoming Oil and Gas Commission; and the states of Alaska, California, Colorado, New Mexico, Nevada, and Utah. The BLM also gave a presentation on the rule this past May at the Interstate Oil and Gas Compact Commission's meeting. As discussed above, some activities that would actually implement the rule have been temporarily paused as a result of litigation, but BLM intends to resume them at the appropriate time.

Similarly, communication with industry has also been ongoing, but has been paused to the extent consistent with the Court's order. Our offices have reached out to local or regional industry organizations and local operators to address their questions related to the implementation process. On April 7, 2015, BLM Washington hosted a nationwide industry outreach session that over 200 people participated in to explain the rule and answer questions about its implementation. Since that time, similar sessions have been held or set up at the local level. BLM state and field offices have coordinated and held training opportunities with associations representing producers in Wyoming, Utah, Colorado, Montana, and North Dakota. Finally, we are also working closely with the Ground Water Protection Council (GWPC) to finalize a MOU that will ensure that the chemical disclosures provided by industry can be easily searched and downloaded from the GWPC's publicly available hydraulic fracturing database, FracFocus.

LEGAL CHALLENGES TO THE RULE

As you know, two industry associations (Independent Petroleum Association of America and the Western Energy Alliance) and a number of the states (Wyoming, Colorado, North Dakota, and Utah), and the Ute Tribe of the Uintah and Ouray Reservation have challenged the rule in the U.S. District Court in Wyoming. The Sierra Club and five other environmental organizations have intervened in that litigation to defend the rule. A separate suit was filed by the Southern Ute Indian Tribe in the U.S. District Court in Colorado. These suits are still in the early phases, and we are vigorously defending the rule and strongly believe it is clearly and fully consistent with the applicable legal authorities and consistent with the BLM's statutory obligations.

In the Wyoming litigation, the court held a hearing on June 23, 2015, on the motions of several of petitioners for a preliminary injunction. At the end of 6½ hours of testimony and argument, the court did not issue a preliminary injunction against the rule. The court did, however, postpone the effective date of the rule until the administrative record is filed by the BLM, the parties annotate their briefs with citations to the record, and the court has time to render a decision on the preliminary injunction motions. In the Colorado litigation, the court has denied the

Southern Ute tribe's motion for a temporary restraining order, and has set a schedule for litigation going forward.

The BLM has been working diligently with other offices of the Department and with a contractor to prepare and file the administrative record with the Wyoming and Colorado courts, which is currently due to be filed on July 22, 2015, and August 24, 2015, respectively. In the meantime, the rule remains on hold consistent with the Wyoming Court's order until record is filed.

CONCLUSION

The BLM's hydraulic fracturing rule provides a much-needed update to the BLM's existing regulations. It establishes common-sense standards governing modern hydraulic fracturing operations that reflect the technological advancement of the process over time. It also provides opportunities for the BLM to coordinate standards and processes with states and tribes to reduce administrative costs and improve efficiency. These new regulations are essential to our efforts to protect the environment and local communities, while also ensuring the continued conscientious development of our Federal oil and gas resources. Thank you for the opportunity to present this testimony. I will be pleased to answer any questions you may have.

———

Dr. FLEMING. Thank you, Mr. Kornze.

The Chair now recognizes Mr. Olguin for 5 minutes, sir.

STATEMENT OF JAMES M. "MIKE" OLGUIN, COUNCIL MEMBER, SOUTHERN UTE INDIAN TRIBE, IGNACIO, COLORADO

Mr. OLGUIN. Good morning, Chairman Fleming, Ranking Member Lowenthal, and members of the subcommittee. My name is Mike Olguin. I am a member of the Southern Ute Indian Tribal Council, and on behalf of the Southern Ute Indian Tribe, I am honored to be here. With me today are my fellow tribal council member Tyson Thompson; our tribe's legal counsel, Tom Shipps; and the operating director of the Tribe's growth fund, Bob Zahradnik, who is also an experienced petroleum engineer. I may need to call upon them later for help in answering some of your questions.

At this time, Mr. Chairman, I would like to mention a few key items from my written statement, and then, with the possible assistance of my colleagues, I would like to answer questions that you and members of the subcommittee may have.

First, I believe it is important for you to know something about our reservation. The Southern Ute Indian Reservation is located in southwestern Colorado. It is a checkerboard reservation. That is, there are multiple types of landownership within the reservation, including tribal land and non-Indian land. Our reservation is blessed with substantial natural gas resources, and we have relied upon natural gas revenues for more than 50 years to fund our government, care for our members, and preserve our cultural identity.

In 1974, our chairman, Leonard C. Burch, imposed a moratorium on the tribe's oil and gas leasing, because he did not trust the Department of the Interior's oversight. For almost 10 years, that moratorium remained in place. During that time, the tribe established its own energy department, and assembled detailed information about its resources. Only after the tribe felt confident that it could prudently monitor the development of its resources, did leasing recommence.

While Federal laws and regulations continue to require BIA and BLM approval of many oil and gas activities on the Tribe's lands, our own departments have far outstripped the capacity of those

Federal agencies to oversee those activities. Over the course of the last 50 years, oil and gas on our reservation has involved the drilling and hydraulic fracturing of thousands of wells. Throughout that period, there has never been an instance in which hydraulic fracturing has resulted in contamination of usable water resources.

Second, my testimony summarizes our efforts to consult with the BLM with respect to the proposed hydraulic fracturing regulation. Frankly, when the rule was initially considered, the BLM did not take its effect on tribes as a serious issue. By the time the BLM proposed a revised rule in 2013, the BLM recognized that energy-producing tribes had serious concerns with what was being proposed, and it went through the motions of tribal consultation.

Our comments throughout the 4-year process reflected our concern that every extra regulatory step, every extra required report, and every extra approval imposed by the BLM and operators in Indian Country increases the cost of operating on Indian lands, and decreases the ability to attract energy development dollars to our lands.

Simply put, tribal lands are different from public lands. Congress has recognized tribal rights of self-governance over tribal lands. We repeatedly called upon the BLM to separate its regulation of public lands from tribal lands to address those important distinctions. However, the BLM ignored our repeated requests and, in doing so, has embarked on a policy that sets back concepts of tribal sovereignty and self-governance for years.

Third, notwithstanding BLM's refusal to grant tribes an opt-out mechanism, the Southern Ute Tribal Council has adopted its own hydraulic fracturing rule. Under existing Bureau of Indian Affairs regulations, we maintain that the Southern Ute rule supersedes the BLM final rule as to lands within the tribe's jurisdiction. Frankly, our rule is a better rule. It eliminate BLM's pre-approval delays and interpretive exercises, but imposes more demanding cementing requirements on operators. It provides certainty.

Fourth, my testimony informs the subcommittee that our tribe has commenced a lawsuit in Federal court in Denver, challenging the lawfulness of the BLM final rule as it applies to our lands. We believe the BLM's failure to recognize tribal sovereignty in its regulation violates the letter and the spirit of the Indian Reorganization Act of 1934, and Congress' tribal mineral leasing statutes.

In conclusion, Mr. Chairman, the Southern Ute Indian Tribe has consistently been a leader in energy development and environmental protection. The BLM's effort to lump tribal lands and public lands into a one-size-fits-all basket is poor policy. Our sovereign rights to manage and protect our own lands are simply too important to turn over to the BLM, and we do not intend to do so. Thank you.

[The prepared statement of Mr. Olguin follows:]

PREPARED STATEMENT OF HON. JAMES M. "MIKE" OLGUIN, SOUTHERN UTE INDIAN TRIBAL COUNCIL MEMBER, SOUTHERN UTE INDIAN TRIBE

I. INTRODUCTION

Chairman Lamborn, Ranking Member Lowenthal and members of the subcommittee, I am Mike Olguin, an elected member of the Southern Ute Indian Tribal Council, which is the governing body of the Southern Ute Indian Tribe. I am honored to appear before you to provide testimony regarding the future of hydraulic fracturing regulation on federally managed lands, including Indian lands. For approximately 4 years, our tribe has actively opposed the Bureau of Land Management's attempt to lump Indian lands and public lands into a "one-size-fits-all" basket for purposes of approving and regulating hydraulic fracturing. To the unnecessary detriment of our tribal government, which relies upon energy related revenue, we believe the BLM's approval requirements are poorly conceived. In order to nullify the BLM's regulatory efforts on our tribe's lands, we have exercised our sovereign rights by enacting our own hydraulic fracturing regulation. The Southern Ute regulation ensures prudent, environmentally sound practices in a much more reasonable and efficient manner than the BLM's rule. Our tribal leaders hope that your intervention in the hydraulic fracturing debate will lead to respectful recognition of Indian tribal sovereignty in regulating activities on their own lands, regardless of executive or legislative policy decisions applicable to Federal public lands.

II. BACKGROUND

The Southern Ute Indian Reservation consists of approximately 700,000 acres of land located in southwestern Colorado in the Four Corners Region of the United States. Our Reservation is part of the northern San Juan Basin, an area that has seen widespread oil and gas development over a period of almost 70 years. The revenues we receive from natural gas development of tribal lands on our Reservation are the tribe's economic lifeblood. For decades, we have worked with industry and with Federal agencies to ensure that oil and gas development occurs in an environmentally responsible manner on our lands.

The landownership pattern within our Reservation is complex and includes parcels of tribal trust lands, parcels of allotted lands owned by individual Indians, parcels owned by non-Indians, Federal lands and state lands. In many situations, non-Indian mineral estates are adjacent to tribal mineral estates. This landownership pattern is significant and magnifies the impact of differences between Federal regulation of Indian lands and state regulation of neighboring non-Indian lands. The burden of unnecessary Federal regulation provides a direct incentive for operators to lease and drill on offsetting non-Indian lands and to avoid development of tribal energy resources. The disincentive to develop tribal energy resources includes ever-increasing fees for processing Applications for Permits to Drill ("APDs") and permit delays. The burden of Federal regulation results in lost revenue to our tribe, as well as potential drainage of tribal minerals.

Hydraulic fracturing involves the underground injection of fluid and proppants under high pressure in order to propagate and maintain fractures and enhance the movement and recovery of oil and gas. Hydraulic fracturing is necessary for the continued development of energy resources from sandstones, shales and coal formations on our lands. Thousands of wells on our Reservation have been stimulated through hydraulic fracturing of sandstones and coalbeds. Preliminary studies also indicate that there are significant recoverable reserves associated with shale formations underlying our Reservation that will require hydraulic fracturing in order to be produced.

Over the course of the extensive history of hydraulic fracturing on our Reservation, there have been no documented cases of adverse environmental impacts resulting from such well stimulation. It should be noted that the hydrocarbon bearing zones on our Reservation are generally located at depths much greater (2,500 to 8,000 feet below surface) than usable water aquifers (typically 100 to 300 feet below surface). Further, the hydrocarbon bearing zones are separated from usable aquifers by thick strata with low permeability. Even with those natural safeguards in place, our tribe has led the effort to ensure that oil and gas development activities do not adversely affect surface or groundwater resources. Significantly, in the course of reviewing APDs on our lands, we have insisted upon regular Bradenhead testing of well integrity and have required cementing of well casings to surface.

In recent years, oil and gas companies have been able to recover oil and gas resources throughout the country from shales and tight formations previously considered unproductive. Technological advances in horizontal drilling and hydraulic fracturing stimulation spurred these resource recovery opportunities. The significant expansion of this activity into geographic areas not previously subject to oil and gas development has fostered debate regarding the environmental effects of hydraulic fracturing. These concerns have, in turn, led the Department of the Interior and the BLM to develop a response intended to ensure the public that, through government oversight and regulation, hydraulic fracturing occurring on Federal and Indian leased lands will be undertaken in an environmentally safe and prudent manner. While this goal may appear reasonable, the process employed by the BLM in developing the regulations applicable to Indian lands was flawed and the ultimate set of regulations is objectionable.

III. THE PROCESS OF CONSULTATION WITH AFFECTED INDIAN TRIBES WAS INADEQUATE

A. *The Initial Proposed Rule*

In mid-December of 2011, BLM's Assistant Director for Minerals and Realty Management Michael D. Nedd, sent a letter inviting our tribe and other tribes to engage in government-to-government consultation regarding BLM's intent to develop regulations governing hydraulic fracturing on Federal and Indian lands. We welcomed this initial invitation for early consultation. On January 19, 2012, a substantial contingent of our tribe's staff, including representatives from our Energy Department, Natural Resources Department, and Environmental Programs Division, attended a BLM information session in Farmington, New Mexico, where representatives from the BLM provided basic information about hydraulic fracturing and asked for tribal input regarding the shape that any such regulations might take. We congratulated BLM on this seemingly fresh approach to visiting with tribes at the formative stages of regulation development. We also delivered at that time written comments from our now deceased Chairman, the late Jimmy R. Newton, Jr., that addressed three principal matters: (1) suggestions for process; (2) a summary of the importance of hydraulic fracturing to the tribe; and (3) a summary of potential environmental concerns and protection measures associated with hydraulic fracturing.

In commenting on process, Chairman Newton's letter specifically urged that "the consultation process include not only an opportunity to comment on proposed BLM regulations but consultation on the formulation of proposed regulations." Chairman Newton further suggested that "BLM circulate discussion drafts of possible regulations for review and comment before any proposed regulations are issued." Only later did we learn that our concept of meaningful tribal consultation had been short-changed from the outset by the BLM. Notwithstanding our requests and suggestions, BLM proceeded to develop draft proposed regulations in isolation and, without disclosing its activities to tribes, submitted those draft regulations to the Office of Management and Budget for publication approval in the *Federal Register*. This process truly was an example of the Federal trustee's train having left the station before Indian Country had a chance to know that the train was even moving. Within a month following BLM's publication of the proposed regulation, we submitted written comments to the BLM on June 11, 2012, and expressed our deep concerns with many of the substantive proposals contained in those draft regulations. Our comments at that time reflected our ongoing concern that every extra regulatory step, every extra required report, and every extra approval imposed by the Federal Government on operators in Indian Country increases the costs of operating in Indian Country and decreases the ability of tribes to attract energy development dollars to our lands.

B. *The Revised Proposed Rule*

In response to over 177,000 comments, the BLM issued a revised proposed rule on May 24, 2013. Again, our tribe weighed into the discussion, not just by submitting written comments, but by meeting with key officials within the Department of the Interior, the BLM, the Bureau of Indian Affairs ("BIA"), and the White House. Among our substantive comments to the revised proposed rule, we questioned the cost effectiveness of the BLM's approval requirements; its capacity to interpret cement evaluation logs and cement bond logs; its approach to isolation of geologic zones containing unusable groundwater; and the vague—but broad—discretion retained by the BLM to impose potentially unlimited conditions on hydraulic fracturing activities without any established time frames for issuing approval. Most significantly, we urged the BLM to separate its rulemaking on public lands from Indian lands. In calling for that separation, we emphasized the dramatic differences in Federal law and policy underpinning Federal public lands and Indian lands, which had spawned separate regulatory regimes for Indian mineral leasing, royalty valuation and collection, and pooling and unitization of subsurface resources, as well as empowerment of tribes in implementing key environmental laws. Further, we specifically reminded the BLM that, under long-established regulations governing Indian mineral leasing, tribes organized under the Indian Reorganization Act of 1934 ("IRA"), like the Southern Ute Indian Tribe, retained the authority to supersede the BIA's mineral leasing regulations, including incorporated BLM regulations made applicable to tribal lands. *See* 25 C.F.R. § 211.29. In its explanation of the revised proposed rule, however, the BLM stated that Congress had tied its hands and that it lacked the authority to separate tribal lands and public lands in developing the proposed rule. In response, we stated as follows:

> For the BLM to suggest that it lacks the power to consider tribal lands and public land distinctly defies decades of statutory and regulatory treatment and is, frankly, insulting. Rather, the proper question is whether there is any reason to treat such lands differently, and, if reasonable grounds are provided for such different treatment, then the BLM should strive to do so.

See Comment Letter from Chairman Jimmy R. Newton, Jr. to BLM at 4 (Aug. 20, 2013).

As the subcommittee is fully aware, on March 26, 2015, the Assistant Secretary for Land and Minerals Management, Janice M. Schneider, approved the BLM's final rule regulating hydraulic fracturing on Federal and Indian lands. 80 Fed. Reg. 16128.

IV. THE TRIBE'S HYDRAULIC FRACTURING REGULATION

On June 16, 2015, the Southern Ute Indian Tribal Council adopted Resolution No. 2015–98, which approved the tribe's regulation of hydraulic fracturing and chemical disclosure on lands within the jurisdiction of the tribe. As authorized by 25 C.F.R. § 211.29, the tribe's regulation expressly states that it supersedes the BLM's regulation. I will briefly summarize the key differences between the Southern Ute rule and the BLM rule. Under the Southern Ute rule, an operator must provide the Southern Ute Department of Energy 48 hours advance written notice of its intent to conduct hydraulic fracturing operations. The Tribe's Department of Energy may review operator information related to the proposed activity and may monitor that activity. Following the completion of hydraulic fracturing, the operator must provide the tribe with a detailed report describing the activities. In order to ensure that hydraulic fracturing occurs in an environmentally sound manner, an operator is required to cement all surface and intermediate casing with a continuous column from the bottom of that casing to the surface, and all production casing must be cemented from the bottom of the vertical portion of the production casing to at least 50 feet above the bottom of the intermediate casing. In that regard, the Southern Ute rule is more restrictive than the BLM rule or the state of Colorado's cementing requirements. The Southern Ute rule provides a better safeguard to water quality and greater certainty to operators, while also eliminating the delays inherent in pre-approval. Like the BLM rule, however, the tribe's rule also requires storage of wastewater in tanks and the public disclosure of the chemical composition hydraulic fracturing fluids.

In contrast, under the BLM rule an operator must obtain BLM *pre-approval* before the operator may proceed with hydraulic fracturing activities. There is no time period following submission of such an application within which BLM must issue its approval or disapproval. In granting approval, the BLM has the discretion to impose a wide variety of conditions, including the imposition of discretionary conditions that exceed those explicitly required in the rule. Critically, unlike the tribe's straight forward cementing requirement, the BLM rule's cementing requirement is based upon the isolation of zones that contain usable water, which requires an interpretive water quality analysis. In addition to the inherent delay associated with securing discretionary agency approval, the act of approval for each well arguably triggers the need for a separate analysis under the National Environmental Policy Act ("NEPA"), which invites additional delays through third-party challenges and potential litigation by those opposed to oil and gas development.

In sum, we strongly believe that the Southern Ute rule provides a simpler and more effective way to regulate hydraulic fracturing activity on the tribe's lands than the BLM rule.

V. SOUTHERN UTE INDIAN TRIBE V. DEPARTMENT OF THE INTERIOR

On June 18, 2015, several days before the BLM rule was to become effective, the Southern Ute Indian Tribe filed a lawsuit in the U.S. District Court for the District of Colorado. *Southern Ute Indian Tribe* v. *United States Department of the Interior, et al.*, Civil Action No. 1:15–cv–01303–MSK (D. Colo). In that case, the tribe has challenged the lawfulness of the rule, including its failure to recognize an IRA tribe's unconditional right to supersede the BLM final rule. We have also asserted that the rule should be vacated as arbitrary and unreasonable in its treatment of Indian tribes, whose powers of self-governance under statutes and policies have been repeatedly emphasized over the last 40 years. The tribe's opening brief on the lawfulness challenge is due on July 23, 2015, and oral argument is scheduled for October 14, 2015.

CONCLUSION

In conclusion, I am honored to appear before you today on behalf of the Southern Ute Indian Tribe. We recognize that your work involves broad oversight of BLM's role in energy development on public lands, and that energy development on Indian lands is not a matter on which you typically focus. To the extent you can do so, however, we hope that you will assist us in preserving our sovereign rights to regulate activities on our lands. We also hope that the common-sense approach that we have taken with respect to our lands will assist you and the BLM in fashioning a reasonable approach to hydraulic fracturing regulation on Federal public lands. We look forward to continuing our work with the subcommittee on this and other important matters.

At this point, I would be happy to answer any questions you may have.

———

Dr. FLEMING. Thank you, Mr. Olguin.

The Chair now recognizes Mr. Hetrick to testify for 5 minutes.

STATEMENT OF LLOYD HETRICK, OPERATIONS ENGINEERING ADVISOR, NEWFIELD EXPLORATION COMPANY, THE WOODLANDS, TEXAS

Mr. HETRICK. Congressman Fleming, Ranking Member Lowenthal, and distinguished members of this subcommittee, my name is Lloyd Hetrick. I am a professional engineer, and an operations engineering advisor for Newfield Exploration Company. Thank you for inviting me to testify today.

The future of hydraulic fracturing and, therefore, oil and gas development on federally managed lands is uncertain. Every day, independent oil and gas companies like Newfield make key decisions on where to invest our drilling capital. We evaluate not only the potential quantity and quality of natural resources available, but also the regulatory uncertainties that may impede our ability to bring them to market economically.

From new hydraulic fracturing regulations to additional air, water, and endangered species initiatives, Federal lands carry extra burdens when competing for our investment dollars. This should concern policymakers of every stripe, because the public's oil and gas resources are among the Nation's largest sources of non-tax revenue for the Federal Government.

For every dollar the government spends administering the Federal onshore program, companies return over $83 in royalties, rents, bonuses, and other revenue to the taxpayer. Every barrel of crude and Mcf of natural gas produced here in America, and each dollar that flows to the U.S. Treasury from activity on federally managed lands, provides lawmakers with additional foreign policy and budget options.

We live in an era of energy abundance, where the combined technologies of horizontal drilling and hydraulic fracturing have been unlocked, and oil and gas resources thought to be uneconomic for development less than a decade ago are now commercially developed. But such promise can be stifled by regulation run amuck. My testimony today details a few of these amucks created by the BLM's new hydraulic fracturing rule, including: it impacts non-Federal lands, most significantly in the western United States, the checkerboard pattern referenced earlier, and other parts of the United States also.

It additionally creates inefficiencies not properly addressed in the BLM's economic analysis. It duplicates, in some cases contradicts, and increases confusion with respect to existing state regulations. And, finally, it uses the public as a secondary regulator. This will create new challenges for both the BLM and the operator, and add confusion to the public.

If the committee intends to create more certainty with regard to the future of hydraulic fracturing and, therefore, oil and gas development on federally managed lands and those state and private lands that are also impacted by this rule should the courts allow the rule to move forward, then I respectfully request the committee help the BLM to improve it.

Finally, I do want to recognize my peers in the BLM for reaching out to all stakeholders during this process since early 2012. They have listened to concerns from all sides, and attempted to find reasonable middle ground. My arguments presented today are not intended as an indictment of the agency, rather a reflection of the complexity of this rulemaking process.

Thank you for this opportunity, and I look forward to your questions.

[The prepared statement of Mr. Hetrick follows:]

PREPARED STATEMENT OF LLOYD H. HETRICK, NEWFIELD EXPLORATION COMPANY

Chairman Lamborn, Ranking Member Lowenthal and distinguished members of the committee, my name is Lloyd Hetrick. I am a registered professional engineer and the Operations Engineering Advisor for Newfield Exploration Company based in The Woodlands, Texas.

I have more than 36 years of diverse experience spanning all phases of the exploration and production industry, including: drilling, completions, production, Health, Safety and Environmental (HSE), and mechanical integrity. I have served a leadership role in the standard setting process for hydraulic fracturing via multiple Federal agency advisory panels and industry trade association committees working to develop and implement appropriate governmental regulations and standards.

Thank you for having me here today.

Newfield is a Fortune 500 independent energy company engaged primarily in crude oil and natural gas exploration and production onshore here in the United States. We are focused on developing unconventional oil and gas reservoirs in the Anadarko and Arkoma Basins of Oklahoma, the Bakken formations of North Dakota and the Uinta Basin of Utah. Roughly 55 percent of our wells drilled domestically during 2014 were administered by the Bureau of Land Management (BLM).

Newfield is the largest oil producer in Utah with more than 225,000 mineral acres in the Uinta Basin including Federal, state, tribal and private leases. Our Uinta Basin operations include one of the largest Federal secondary recovery units in the continental United States. We maintain a field office near Roosevelt, Utah, with more than 400 employees. Approximately 85 percent of our wells drilled in Utah during 2014 were administered by BLM.

All of our Utah development activities—regardless if conducted on Federal, state, tribal or private leases—will ultimately be affected by BLM's new hydraulic fracturing rule. As I'll discuss further, there is no practical scenario in which Newfield can hold its state or private leases to a different standard than its Federal or tribal leases and coherently manage a compliance program in its Utah operations.

Therefore, this rule impacts everything we do in Utah and adds significant uncertainty and cost to an already low-margin resource play to further complicate the future of hydraulic fracturing on federally managed lands.

The recent downturn in global crude oil prices has resulted in a reduction of Newfield's investment and workforce in the Uinta Basin and has impacted peer companies similarly—significantly impacting the employment of local contractors and related commerce. At this same time last year, there were 28 rigs running in Utah; today, there are 7. The economic realities of production in Utah are further undermined by the BLM rule.

This reduction in drilling and production has and will continue to adversely affect employment, wages, Federal royalties, taxes and all of the related socioeconomic benefits enjoyed during times of robust development.

It is important to remember that every $1 million of upstream capital expenditure by independent oil and gas producers results in $1.1 million in total taxes, $5.1 million in overall contribution to U.S. GDP and 6 direct and 33 total upstream jobs. When midstream and downstream factors are considered, America's oil and gas industry supports 9.2 million U.S. jobs and 7.7 percent of the Nation's GDP according to the American Petroleum Institute. The industry pays almost $86 million in Federal rents, royalties, bonus payments and income tax payments *daily*.

Revenue in the form of royalties, rents, bonuses and other payments to American Indian tribes nationwide for the production of oil and gas in FY2014 was reported by the Office of Natural Resource Revenue (ONRR) to be more than $1.1 billion.

America's oil and gas resources are among the Nation's largest sources of non-tax revenue to the Federal Government. For every dollar the government spends administering the Federal onshore program, companies return $83.69 in royalties and leasing revenue to the American taxpayer.

From Utah's Federal onshore lands for Fiscal Year 2014, the ONRR reported oil and natural gas revenue in the form of royalties, rents, bonuses, and other payments to the U.S. Treasury in excess of $302 million.

Unfortunately, the decline Utah activity has already occurred and may continue to negatively impact Utah and especially the Uinta Basin for the foreseeable future.

In addition to the negative economic effects caused by the downturn in crude oil prices, significant regulatory uncertainty already existed for Newfield and other Uinta Basin operators due to the lack of predictability associated with agency reviews mandated by the National Environmental Policy Act (NEPA). While outside the scope of this hearing, it is worth mentioning as an example that Newfield is now in its seventh year of agency review for an infill development Environmental Impact Statement (EIS).

BLM's hydraulic fracturing regulation creates an additional layer of regulatory uncertainty that will materially undermine the ability of the Uinta Basin to compete on an economic basis with other plays in the Nation. When any operator is faced with such uncertainty, capital and resources will be redirected to areas where the regulatory process is more certain. This was not anticipated in the rulemaking process and is discussed further below.

I will not dwell on often-recited and *legitimate* arguments by industry that this new rule is unnecessary because of sufficient and continually improving state regulations and lacks appropriate data to justify these new rules. I would however, like to remind the committee of the EPA's finding of "no widespread, systematic impacts" from hydraulic fracturing in their recently released "Assessment of the Potential Impacts of Hydraulic Fracturing for Oil and Gas on Drinking Water Resources."

I respectfully offer the committee three categories of concerns and include Newfield-specific examples to support my assertion that if this new BLM regulation is to be implemented, it still needs more work.

I want to recognize my peers at BLM for reaching out to all stakeholders during the rulemaking process. Since 2012, BLM has listened to concerns from all sides and—to a large extent—attempted to find reasonable middle ground. The following arguments are not an indictment of the agency nor of those who have worked to craft the rule in response to direction from more senior political leadership, rather they reflect the complexity of this process.

The BLM rule, in many cases, impacts non-Federal minerals, causes delays and creates inefficiencies that were not properly addressed in the BLM's economic analysis:

- For operations located in certain BLM regions like North Dakota and Montana operators with state or private leases that are combined within a drilling and spacing unit also including Federal minerals, the entire unit becomes subject to the new rule. Other BLM regions such as Utah and Oklahoma limit the extent of the new rule to apply only when the Federal tract is penetrated by the wellbore within the drilling and spacing unit.
- With most unconventional oil and gas plays in which horizontal extended reach wells are utilized to properly develop the lands, drilling and spacing units tend to be larger than the conventional vertical units and encompass more lands within the development drilling and spacing unit. Therefore, previously non-applicable minerals are more likely to fall under this new BLM rule. This particular scenario is most clearly demonstrated with the "checkerboard" Federal mineral ownership pattern common across the western United

States. Although only 50 percent of the checkerboard has Federal minerals, 100 percent of the checkerboard becomes subject to the new rule. A similar, but more dramatic scenario exists in Newfield's Oklahoma operations where a small amount of Federal minerals causes a much larger area to become Federal jurisdiction. Roughly 1 percent of our Anadarko position is Federal minerals, yet even with this small subset of Federal minerals, the new rule will apply to more than 10 times that amount. Neither the Federal checkerboard nor the Oklahoma example was contemplated in BLM's new rule.

- In some instances, inadequate cementing records or some potential technical disagreement on Cement Evaluation Log (CEL) interpretation—not a shortfall in well integrity—may result in a new well that cannot be hydraulically fractured or an existing well than cannot be refractured. The cost of such a problem ranges from a few hours of lost operational downtime up to the cost of a $10 million well.
- Specific to the downtime referenced above, every hydraulic fracturing job requires at least a 48-hour notice to obtain BLM approval of cement-related assurances. However, BLM is barely staffed to provide support during a normal 40-hour work week, certainly not 24/7/365 support.
- Finally, the Office of the Inspector General has recognized that inefficiencies in the Department of Interior's permit review process impede productivity and that neither BLM nor the operator can predict when permits will be approved. Since site-specific operational plans cannot often be finalized months in advance, operators may be forced to submit applications that include multiple scenarios to ensure operational flexibility. Although some of the proposed operational scenarios may never be implemented, an already overburdened BLM staff will be required to review all components of the new applications.

This rule has portions that duplicate, contradict or increase confusion with respect to existing state regulations, or in some cases, presents perplexing requirements:

- Duplication—Surface casing cementing rules are essentially the same in the new BLM rule as are required in all oil and gas producing states.
- Contradiction—The new BLM rule requires pressure measurement on all casing strings during hydraulic fracturing, but the North Dakota Industrial Commission requires the surface annulus to be kept open to protect the surface casing and provide pressure relief, in case a leak occurs.
- Deferral with Uncertainty—The BLM rule says *all* usable water must be protected and further defers the identification of what "usable water" must be protected to states and tribes. This deferral is unambiguous as long as states and tribes use a threshold of 10,000 mg/l TDS, but not all states use this threshold, nor do all states protect *all* usable water. Please remember that "usable" does not necessarily mean "useful" to plants, wildlife or humans.
- Deferral with Uncertainty—BLM recognizes the use of FracFocus for chemical disclosure, but adds additional onerous steps which limit a company's ability to protect trade secrets and inhibits innovation in this technology-driven part of our business.
- Perplexing—The BLM rule requires that operators make seven illogical affirmations in order to claim trade secret protection when providing public disclosure for proprietary chemicals used during hydraulic fracturing.
- Perplexing—The BLM rule requires a certification that attests to a company's compliance with all Federal, state and local laws, rules and regulations. However, with increased local challenges and initiatives, this certification might be impossible to achieve without a time and date stamp.

The BLM's strategy to use public review as a secondary regulator will create foreseeable challenges for BLM and the operator and confusion for the public:

- BLM's *stated* incremental processing time for each new well application is only 4 hours, so there cannot be much technical analysis planned for the significant amount of new information submitted.
- Considering BLM statements that public access to this information will be facilitated, it appears BLM is promoting several predictable outcomes:
  —The public will be reviewing substantial technical and specialized industry information, of which many will not be familiar. Confusion about the

technologies or the processes required to effectively achieve desired environmental and safety outcomes will result in further questions of, and petitions to, BLM and operators.

—The predictable outcome will be a further-inundated regulator while the operator is faced with the ongoing task of educating the public that hydraulic fracturing has been, and will continue to be a safe well completion technique for almost seven decades.

—In short, the rule will have failed to provide the public with assurances about the safety of hydraulic fracturing technology while adding delays, costs, and uncertainty for industry and consumers.

In conclusion, if this final BLM rule is to be applied, additional actions need to be taken to provide an economic analysis, operational clarifications and a fundamental clarification on the role of the BLM as the primary regulator for Federal and tribal minerals.

Finally, Newfield wishes to associate itself with any written testimony submitted to the committee on this topic by the Independent Petroleum Association of America, the Western Energy Alliance, or the American Exploration & Production Council.

————

Dr. FLEMING. Thank you, Mr. Hetrick.

The Chair now recognizes Ms. Wiseman to testify for 5 minutes.

STATEMENT OF HANNAH WISEMAN, ATTORNEYS' TITLE PROFESSOR, FLORIDA STATE UNIVERSITY COLLEGE OF LAW, TALLAHASSEE, FLORIDA

Ms. WISEMAN. Acting Chairman Fleming, Ranking Member Lowenthal, and members of the committee, I thank you for the opportunity to appear before you today. I speak for myself alone. But solely by way of background, I have taught several environmental law and oil and gas law classes at the University of Texas School of Law, University of Tulsa School of Law, and I am currently at the Florida State University College of Law.

I will speak today about the authority of the Bureau of Land Management to issue the final rule, entitled, "Oil and Gas: Hydraulic Fracturing on Federal and Indian Lands." I will also describe how this rule is not precluded by other Federal statutes, how it addresses known risks, and how it beneficially complements existing state and tribal programs.

In 1920, the Secretary of the Interior regulated the casing of oil and gas wells on Federal lands under the Mineral Leasing Act. In 1942, the U.S. Geological Survey, the BLM's predecessor in regulating wells on Federal lands, promulgated regulations allowing requirements for well casing programs and well stimulation plans to be submitted prior to the injection of water, acid, or other substances. The BLM has since issued a variety of regulations for oil and gas development.

The HF rule provides a needed update to BLM rules, in light of the relatively new combination technique of slick water fracturing and horizontal drilling. The BLM has ample authority under either the Federal Land Policy and Management Act or the Mineral Leasing Act, in addition to the Indian Mineral Leasing Act and other acts, to issue this rule.

It is the policy of the Federal Land Policy and Management Act to protect environmental, ecological, and "water resource" values, and to promote multiple-use development of lands. Beyond this baseline requirement, the MLA, the Mineral Leasing Act, prohibits the waste of oil and gas, and directs the BLM to conserve surface resources. It authorizes the BLM to do any and all things necessary to carry out the Act's purposes.

The BLM rule also addresses known risks. Some unconventional wells have had deficient casing, as indicated by state inspectors' reports. Methane has leaked to the surface in some cases. Fracturing fluid and flowback stored on well sites has leaked and run off sites, as described on pages 6–7 of my testimony. Other Federal environmental statutes do not preclude or displace BLM regulation of fracturing and associated well activities.

When several Federal statutes potentially apply to an activity, the question is whether Congress indicated an intent for one statute to preclude the others. The Safe Drinking Water Act, which exempts hydraulic fracturing with the exception of diesel fuel, indicates no intent to preclude regulation of fracturing, casing, or cementing on Federal lands. The exemption is only for purposes of this part. The legislative history of the Act also states that Congress did not intend to limit the authority of BLM's predecessor to protect groundwater.

Further, Federal environmental acts like the Safe Drinking Water Act, do not comprehensively address the unique responsibilities of Federal agencies to protect public natural resources. Those responsibilities are addressed under acts like the Federal Land Policy and Management Act and the Mineral Leasing Act.

Finally, with respect to the interaction of state, tribal, and Federal regulations on BLM lands, the BLM's rule is more stringent than some state regulations and less stringent than others. Where the BLM rule is less stringent than state regulations, the rule will simply act as a floor above which states are free to regulate more stringently, without any BLM review, as has always been the case. A variance will be unnecessary, although it is an option. Where the rule is more stringent, it will provide a consistent standard for wells drilled on Federal lands.

Wells of the BLM must administer in the public interest. Many of the standards in the HF rule are not one-size-fits-all, and anticipate well-specific determinations. Adding BLM enforcement resources to existing state resources will also be beneficial, providing more feet on the ground for inspections and enforcement. States have done an admirable job of inspecting more sites as development has boomed, as have the tribes. But budget constraints and outdated fee structures at the state level have hindered certain state enforcement efforts.

In summary, the HF rule has strong statutory authorization, is not precluded by other Federal statutes, addresses known risks, and usually complements but in no way displaces state regulation. Thank you.

[The prepared statement of Ms. Wiseman follows:]

PREPARED STATEMENT OF HANNAH J. WISEMAN,[1] ATTORNEYS' TITLE PROFESSOR,
FLORIDA STATE UNIVERSITY COLLEGE OF LAW

INTRODUCTION

This testimony addresses the Bureau of Land Management Final Rule entitled
"Oil and Gas; Hydraulic Fracturing on Federal and Indian Lands" (described here
as the "HF Rule") issued on March 26, 2015.[2] After summarizing key provisions of
the HF Rule, this testimony will describe the authority of the BLM to promulgate
the rule, the lack of conflict between the HF Rule and other Federal statutes, the
environmental risks that the rule helps to address, and the ways in which the HF
Rule and Federal enforcement resources complement and improve upon state
regulation of oil and gas development.

I. RULE SUMMARY: THE HF RULE ADDRESSES CERTAIN ASPECTS OF THE CASING AND
CEMENTING OF HYDRAULICALLY FRACTURED WELLS, THE STORAGE OF FRACTURING
WASTES, AND THE DISCLOSURE OF FRACTURING CHEMICALS

The HF Rule primarily contains requirements for information collection and disclosure, mandating that well operators proposing to hydraulically fracture a well on
Federal or Indian lands submit data on the geology in the proposed area of the
well;[3] existing conditions such as old wells, natural faults and fractures, and usable
water in the area;[4] and proposed hydraulic fracturing design, water acquisition,
waste management, and disposal practices.[5] After fracturing, operators—entities
that drill and hydraulically fracture wells—must disclose data on well depth and
fractures; actual water acquisition, waste management, and disposal practices; and
the chemicals used in fracturing.[6] Operators can avoid public disclosure of certain
chemicals used in the fracturing process by submitting an affidavit to the BLM with
information indicating, *inter alia*, the importance of keeping the information con-
fidential.[7] Operators also must collect data on the quality of cementing operations
to show that the protective casing and cementing of wells is adequate, and they
must monitor the pressure in wells during hydraulic fracturing to ensure that pressures do not compromise the structure ("integrity") of the well and its casing and
cement.[8] Substantive requirements include, *inter alia*, that operators take remedial
action if it appears that well cementing was inadequate or that fracturing compromised well integrity[9] and that operators use tanks to store flowback water from
fracturing, with certain exceptions.[10] Where state or tribal requirements achieve or
exceed the goals of the HF Rule, the BLM may grant a regulation-specific variance
from the BLM rule for all wells in the relevant jurisdiction or for individual wells;[11]
as discussed below, however, these variances may be unnecessary because BLM
rules are a floor, not a ceiling.

II. THE BLM HAS CLEAR STATUTORY AUTHORITY TO REGULATE HYDRAULICALLY
FRACTURED OIL AND GAS WELLS ON FEDERAL LANDS

The BLM permits and oversees the use of Federal lands for a variety of purposes,
including grazing, recreation, and oil and gas development, among other purposes.
In leasing federally-owned oil and gas, the BLM—just like private owners of land
and minerals—must protect the public's interest in the minerals and land and ensure that fluid mineral development will not unduly interfere with other uses of
land. Indeed, many private landowners include conditions in mineral leases in order
to protect their property and natural resources.[12] However, in leasing Federal oil

---

[1] The author thanks Elizabeth Farrell, Mary McCormick, and other Florida State University
College of Law Research Center Directors and Librarians, Shi-Ling Hsu, David Markell, Bruce
Pendery, and Erin Ryan for suggested edits and sources.

[2] Oil and Gas; Hydraulic Fracturing on Federal and Indian Lands, 80 Fed. Reg. 16,128 (Mar.
26, 2015) (to be codified at 43 C.F.R. pt. 3160).

[3] *Id.* at 16,218.

[4] *Id.*

[5] *Id.* at 16,218–16,219.

[6] *Id.* at 16,220–16,221.

[7] *Id.*

[8] *Id.* at 16,219–16,220.

[9] *Id.*

[10] *Id.* at 16,220.

[11] *Id.* at 16,221.

[12] *See, e.g.,* Oil and Gas Lease Between James J. Franko & Nancy L. Franko and Rex Energy
I, LLC, Apr. 22, 2008, *available at* http://www.nytimes.com/interactive/2011/12/02/us/oil-and-gas-
leases.html?_r=0#document/221308-rex20080422fra (requiring testing of water supplies prior to
drilling and replacement of water supplies if supplies are impacted and requiring the payment

and gas resources, the BLM represents broader public interests that diverge from those of most private mineral owners. Resources administered by the BLM are, by law, not managed solely, or even primarily, for pecuniary gain. The BLM's core statutory mandate, contained within the Federal Land Policy and Management Act (FLPMA), is to manage public lands and resources in a manner that allows for multi-use development of lands, including "a combination of balanced and diverse resource uses," [13] by current and future generations of people.[14] Congress has made clear that in managing public resources the BLM must give consideration to "the relative values of the resources and not necessarily to the combination of uses that will give the greatest economic return or the greatest unit output." [15] The BLM therefore must regulate oil and gas development at the surface and belowground to protect its mineral interests and the many other interests that the agency represents on Federal lands, such as grazing and recreational interests. Notably, it is also the express policy of Congress to protect "water resource . . . values" on Federal lands.[16]

FLPMA responsibilities for managing public lands are baseline responsibilities that apply when the BLM leases minerals on public lands. Beyond this baseline law, the BLM must follow the specific directives of the Mineral Leasing Act (MLA), as amended, when it allows mineral development on public lands. This Act provides, *inter alia*, that the Secretary of Interior (whose responsibilities the BLM carries out) must regulate surface-disturbing activities from oil and gas development and ensure "restoration of any lands or surface waters adversely affected by lease operations" by the operator.[17] It also provides that the Secretary of the Interior shall regulate surface disturbing activities and determine reclamation and other actions required "in the interest of conservation of surface resources." [18] Under this Act, the BLM may suspend leases where oil and gas operators have failed to protect the environment.[19] In addition to the BLM's authority under FLPMA, the HF Rule falls clearly within the discretion granted to the BLM by the MLA.[20] Casing and cementing rules prevent oil and gas waste and protect surface (as well as underground) resources, as do rules for the use of flowback tanks.

Federal agencies have long regulated the casing and cementing of wells and other well development activities on public lands. On June 4, 1920, the Secretary of the Interior acting under MLA authority issued operating regulations for oil and gas wells requiring, *inter alia*, notification prior to well drilling, plugging, and abandonment; keeping of records relating to "kinds, length, and sizes of casings used in drilling the wells"; and operator correction of conditions causing damage to water-bearing or other formations or "dangerous to life or property." [21] The U.S. Geological Survey (USGS)—one of the BLM's predecessors in managing wells on public lands—provided in a 1942 regulation that the Supervisor could require the submittal of a well casing program and that drilling, well stimulation, and other well development activities could not occur "without first notifying the supervisor" of a plan.[22]

Many of the BLM's rules for managing mineral resources on Federal lands are more than two decades old, [23] and these rules, like the older USGS rules, have long

---

of damages for impacts to crops and timber). Many other leases in the *New York Times* database contain identical language.

[13] 43 U.S.C. § 1702(c) (2012).

[14] *See* 43 U.S.C. § 1732(a) (2012) (requiring BLM management of public lands "under principles of multiple use and sustained yield"); 43 U.S.C. § 1702(c) (2012) (defining "multiple use" as "the management of the public lands and their various resource values so that they are utilized in the combination that will best meet the present and future needs of the American people").

[15] 43 U.S.C. § 1702(c) (2012).

[16] 43 U.S.C. § 1701(a)(8) (2012).

[17] 30 U.S.C. § 226(g) (2012).

[18] *Id.*

[19] *See Getty Oil v. Clark,* 614 F.Supp. 904, 916 (D. Wyo. 1985) (noting that the Secretary of the DOI may suspend a lease or condition a suspension as is "necessary to protect the environmental values of the leased property").

[20] *See* 30 U.S.C. § 189 (2012) (authorizing the BLM "to do any and all things necessary to carry out and accomplish the purposes of this chapter").

[21] *See Forbes v. United States,* 125 F.2d 404, 409 (9th Cir. 1942) (describing and quoting the regulations).

[22] 30 C.F.R. § 221.21 (1942); Regulations Applicable to Lands of the United States and All Restricted Tribal and Allotted Indian Lands (Except Osage Indian Reservation), 7 Fed. Reg. 4132, 4134–4135 (June 2, 1942).

[23] *See* Molly Feiden, Madeline Gottlieb, Alan Krupnick & Nathan Richardson, *Hydraulic Fracturing on Federal and Indian Lands: An Analysis of the Bureau of Land Management's Revised Proposed Rule,* 29 J. Land Use & Envtl. L. 337, 339 (2013–2014) (noting that most of

Continued

regulated the casing and cementing of oil and gas wells.[24] Yet oil and gas development has changed dramatically in the past decade. U.S. companies have used hydraulic fracturing for more than 60 years,[25] but the type of fracturing used on many wells changed in the late 1990s and early 2000s.[26] During this time George Mitchell perfected a technique called "slickwater" (also called slick water or slick-water) fracturing in Texas' "tight" gas formations, which are densely packed formations, and combined this technique with the horizontal drilling of wells.[27] Several years later, slickwater fracturing and similar unconventional fracturing combined with horizontal drilling rapidly spread around the country to other tight sandstone and shale formations,[28] enabling the development of thousands of new wells drilled into these formations—wells that, without unconventional fracturing and horizontal drilling, would not have been productive and would not have been drilled.[29] Although some oil and gas operators also continue to use conventional fracturing techniques, unconventional fracturing combined with horizontal drilling is very common and has triggered much of the recent boom in U.S. oil and gas development.[30]

The HF Rule, issued after the BLM proposed a draft rule and a revised draft rule[31] and received extensive public comments, addresses certain aspects of modern (unconventional) fracturing on land managed by the BLM, lands under which the BLM controls the minerals, and certain Indian lands.[32] This HF Rule does not exceed the BLM's statutory authority; it has strong statutory support and helps the BLM to fulfill its statutory duties.[33]

FLPMA, the BLM's organic act,[34] declares that it is "the policy of the United States" that "public lands be managed in a manner that will protect the quality of scientific . . . ecological, environmental, air and atmospheric, water resource, and archeological values."[35] It also provides that in administering the Act, the BLM (acting for the Secretary of the Interior, or "Secretary") must "establish *comprehensive* rules and regulations after considering the views of the general public."[36] Congress has set out a specific process for the BLM's leasing and management of Federal oil and gas resources on behalf of the public. Congress directs the Secretary to "manage the public lands under principles of multiple use and sustained yield . . . ,"[37] meaning managing resources "so that they are utilized in the combination that will best meet the present and future needs of the American people" and in

---

the BLM's onshore oil and gas operations regulations "were last revised in the 1980s or early 1990s").

[24] Prior to 2007, the BLM administered an eight-point rule for the casing and cementing of wells on BLM lands. It replaced this with a nine-point rule in 2007. Onshore Oil and Gas Operations; Federal and Indian Oil and Gas Leases; Onshore Oil and Gas Order No. 1, Approval of Operations, 72 Fed. Reg. 10,308, 10,310 (Mar. 7, 2007) (codified at 43 C.F.R. pt. 3160).

[25] See John M. Golden & Hannah J. Wiseman, *The Fracking Revolution: Shale Gas as a Case Study in Innovation Policy*, 64 Emory L.J. 955, 968 (2015) (comparing sources that describe the first fracturing of wells as occurring in the late 1940s).

[26] See Hong Sun et al., *A Nondamaging Friction Reducer for Slickwater Frac Applications*, Soc'y of Petroleum Engineers, Conference Paper no. 139480 at 1 (2011).

[27] See id. at 975 (describing Mitchell's involvement in helping to perfect horizontal drilling and slickwater fracturing). Techniques similar to the slickwater technique, characterized by large quantities of water and fewer gels and other chemicals, had been used in earlier decades but had not been applied to shales and typically had not been combined with horizontal drilling. Experts typically describe slickwater fracturing as a new, recent technology. *See, e.g.,* Terrence Palisch, Michael Vincent & Patrick Handren, *Slickwater Fracturing: Food for Thought*, 25 SPE Production and Operations 327, 327 (2010).

[28] See Golden & Wiseman, *supra* note 25, at 966 ("In the past decade and a half, growth in shale gas production has been more than exponential.").

[29] See, e.g., Halliburton, U.S. Shale Gas: An Unconventional Resource. Unconventional Challenges at 1 (2008), *available at* http://www.shaleenergyinsider.com/wp-content/uploads/sites/11/2014/01/H063771.pdf (noting that the Barnett Shale, investigated "as early as 1981," produced "gas at commercial rates" only when certain fracturing technologies became available).

[30] See U.S. Dept. of Energy, Why Is Shale Gas Important?, http://energy.gov/sites/prod/files/2013/04/f0/why_is_shale_gas_important.pdf (noting that "U.S. shale gas production has increased 12-fold over the last decade" and is projected to make up 49% of U.S. dry natural gas production by 2035). Experts estimated in 2004 that 30% of hydraulic fracturing jobs used slickwater fracturing. Palisch et al., *supra* note 27, at 327.

[31] Oil and Gas; Well Stimulation Including Hydraulic Fracturing, 77 Fed. Reg. 27,691 (proposed May 11, 2012); Supplemental Notice of Proposed Rulemaking and Request for Comment, 78 Fed. Reg. 31,636 (May 24, 2013).

[32] Oil and Gas; Hydraulic Fracturing on Federal and Indian Lands, *supra* note 2.

[33] See infra notes 35–36, 37, and accompanying text.

[34] See New Mexico ex rel. Richardson v. Bureau of Land Management, 565 F.3d 683, 688 n.1 (10th Cir. 2009).

[35] 43 U.S.C. § 1701(a)(12) (2012).

[36] Id. at § 1701(a)(5) (2012) (emphasis added).

[37] Id. at § 1732(a) (2012).

a manner "that takes into account the long-term needs of future generations for renewable and nonrenewable resources, including, but not limited to, recreation, range, timber, minerals, watershed, wildlife and fish, and . . . scientific and historical value." [38] The BLM must write comprehensive land use plans, also described as "resource management plans," [39] and its leasing of oil and gas resources must conform to these plans. [40] If an operator obtains a lease, the operator may apply to the BLM to develop a specific well by submitting an application for a permit to drill (APD). [41]

The BLM has specific regulations that guide its issuance or denial of permits to drill for oil and gas. FLPMA provides: "The Secretary shall issue regulations necessary to implement the provisions of this Act with respect to the management, use, and protection of the public lands, including the property located thereon." [42] Congress also requires that the Secretary "by regulation or otherwise, take any action necessary to prevent unnecessary or undue degradation of the lands" [43] in managing public lands. It is the responsibility of the authorized BLM officer to regulate a host of issues associated with oil and gas drilling quite apart from the HF rule specifically. As provided by BLM regulations, these responsibilities and authorities include, *inter alia*, approving and monitoring operator proposals for drilling, development, or production and ensuring that operations are conducted in a manner that is environmentally responsible, that protects life and property, and that results in the maximum ultimate recovery of the resource with minimum waste. [44] Drilling plans must include "a description of the program, the surface and projected completion zone location, pertinent geologic data, expected hazards, and proposed mitigation measures to address such hazards." [45]

As discussed further below, the HF Rule's requirements, which operate in addition to these other rules, will help to protect groundwater, surface waters, and soils on public lands, thus supporting other current and future uses of BLM lands such as grazing and recreation. By preventing leakage from wells, the requirements will also help to prevent the waste of oil and gas, for which the Federal Government and states receive royalties. [46] Causing waste of oil and gas resources is prohibited by the MLA. [47]

III. THE HF RULE ADDRESSES KNOWN RISKS, PREVENTS THE WASTE OF VALUABLE FEDERAL OIL AND GAS RESOURCES, AND IS NOT OVERLY BURDENSOME

The HF Rule follows Congressional mandates by taking modest steps to address important environmental externalities of oil and gas development and hydraulic fracturing and preventing the waste of Federal mineral resources. Slickwater and other unconventional fracturing techniques that have become common in the past decade, thus necessitating updated BLM rules, use larger volumes of water [48] and in some cases different types of chemicals [49] than other fracturing techniques, and they introduce certain new environmental risks to the oil and gas development process. Beyond causing more wells to be drilled and fractured, sometimes in sensitive environments or more populous areas, [50] slickwater fracturing produces large volumes of liquid "flowback" waste that must be stored on the well site surface and

[38] *Id.* at § 1702(c) (2012).

[39] *See Norton v. Southern Utah Wilderness Alliance*, 542 U.S. 55, 59 (2004); *Pennaco Energy, Inc. v. U.S. Dept. of the Interior*, 377 F.3d 1147, 1151 (10th Cir. 2004).

[40] 43 C.F.R. § 1610.5–3(a) (2013).

[41] *Id.* at § 3162.3–1(c) (2013).

[42] 43 U.S.C. § 1733 (2012).

[43] *Id.* at § 1732(b) (2012)

[44] 43 C.F.R. § 3161.2 (2013).

[45] *Id.* at § 3162.3–1(e).

[46] 30 U.S.C. § 223 (2012); 30 U.S.C. § 191 (2012).

[47] 30 U.S.C. § 225 (2012).

[48] *See, e.g.*, Governor's Marcellus Shale Advisory Commission (Pennsylvania) Report at 73 (2011), http://www.marcellus.psu.edu/resources/PDFs/MSACFinalReport.pdf ("While hydraulic fracturing is not new to the Commonwealth—it has been standard practice for decades—the size of the natural gas play and the quantity of water used to stimulate a Marcellus Shale or other unconventional natural gas well is new.").

[49] *See* Hannah J. Wiseman, *Risk and Response in Fracturing Policy*, 84 U. Colo. L. Rev. 729,744 n. 64 (2013).

[50] *See, e.g.*, City of Fort Worth, Gas Well Drilling, Fortworthtexas.gov, http://fortworthtexas.gov/gaswells/ (last visited July 12, 2015) (showing 1,976 producing gas wells in the City of Fort Worth).

disposed of [51] and requires large volumes of water to be trucked or piped to well sites.[52]

The techniques of hydraulic fracturing (including slickwater fracturing) and horizontal drilling have produced very important economic benefits but also substantial costs—costs that could be reduced through careful management of the drilling and fracturing process. Hydraulic fracturing chemicals, and chemicals mixed with water, have spilled on well sites.[53] Wells have blown out during hydraulic fracturing, causing fracturing fluids to be discharged into surface waters.[54] In its draft assessment of the impacts of hydraulic fracturing on water quality, the Environmental Protection Agency observes that "[s]pills of hydraulic fracturing fluids have occurred across the country and have affected the quality of drinking water resources,"[55] and it estimates that spill rates of chemicals and hydraulic fracturing fluid range from 0.4 and 12.2 spills for every 100 wells."[56] Flowback from wells has also leaked, polluting soil, surface water, and other resources,[57] and, in one incident identified by

---

[51] Envtl. Protection Agency, Assessment of the Potential Impacts, *supra* note 55, at 6–3.

[52] Natl. Park Service, U.S. Dep't of the Interior, Potential Development of the Natural Gas Resources in the Marcellus Shale at 9 (2008), http://www.nps.gov/frhi/learn/management/upload/GRD-M-Shale_12-11-2008_high_res.pdf. Unconventional fracturing techniques can also reduce certain impacts compared to conventional oil and gas production because horizontal drilling makes surface locations more flexible. U.S. Dep't of Energy, Office of Fossil Energy, Environmental Benefits of Advances Oil and Gas Exploration and Production Technology at 5 (1999), http://www.netl.doe.gov/kmd/cds/disk25/oilandgas.pdf.

[53] *See, e.g.*, Dunn Cty., N.D., Well Name Fort Berthold 148–94–22A–27–1H, Incident 20130430182213 (Apr. 30, 2013), http://www.ndhealth.gov/EHS/FOIA/Spills/Summary_Reports/20130430182213_Summary_Report.pdf (spill of 250 barrels of "fracturing solids and liquids"; report indicates 250 barrels were recovered but "[a]dditional soil cleanup on and offsite to continue"); Billings Cty., N.D., Well Name State Hecker 1–2–11H–142–98, Incident 20120614171333 (June 13, 2012), http://www.ndhealth.gov/EHS/FOIA/Spills/Summary_Reports/20120614171333_Summary_Report.pdf (18 barrels of "[f]resh water with fracing chemicals" spilled; 17 barrels cleaned up (recovered); potential environmental impacts to "[s]urface soil only"); Dunn Cty., N.D., Well Name Fuller 1–2H, Incident 20110810153048 (July 20, 2011), http://www.ndhealth.gov/EHS/FOIA/Spills/Summary_Reports/20110810153048_Summary_Report.pdf (release of 8 barrels of "[f]rac water" to a field; "remedial activities" conducted); Lea Cty., N.M., API Permit 30–025–41627, Incident nSAD1413436037 (Apr. 28, 2014), https://www.apps.emnrd.state.nm.us/ocd/ocdpermitting/Data/Incidents/SpillSearchResultsExcel.aspx?Api=30-025-41627 (describing a 7-gallon spill of "hydraulic frac fluid," 6.75 barrels of which were recovered); Eddy Cty., N.M., API Permit 30–015–26415, Incident nMLB1403537703 (Jan. 30, 2014), https://www.apps.emnrd.state.nm.us/ocd/ocdpermitting/Data/Incidents/SpillSearchResultsExcel.aspx?Api=30-015-26415 ("Reported release of 230 bbls fresh water w/2% KCL and gel (for slick water frac job) Released fluids ran down a draw (approx ¼ mile) and entered the Pecos River."); Chaves Cty., N.M., API Permit 30–005–29061, Incident nGRL1010539051 (Feb. 5, 2010), https://www.apps.emnrd.state.nm.us/ocd/ocdpermitting/Data/Incidents/SpillSearchResultsExcel.aspx?Api=30-005-29061 (noting 80 barrels of frac fluid spilled, five of which were recovered).

[54] *See, e.g.*, Md. Att'y Gen., AG Gansler Secures Funding to Safeguard Susquehanna Water Quality (June 14, 2012), http://www.oag.state.md.us/press/2012/061412.html (last visited July 12, 2015) (noting the release of fracturing fluids into Towanda Creek due to a well blowout); Governor's Marcellus Shale Advisory Commission, *supra* note 48, at 75 (noting that "over 10,000 gallons of fracturing flowback fluid escaped the well pad and all containment" in the Towanda Creek incident and describing another blowout that released fracturing fluids for 16 hours); McKenzie Cty., N.D., Well Name Cherry State 31–16H, Incident 20140214142744, (Feb. 13, 2014), http://www.ndhealth.gov/EHS/FOIA/Spills/Summary_Reports/20140214142744_Summary_Report.pdf (describing a blowout at a North Dakota well and noting "[r]egaining well control still in progress"; Nicholas P. Cheremisinoff & Anton R. Davletshin, Hydraulic Fracturing Operations: Handbook of Environmental Management Practices 460 (2015) (indicating that the well in McKenzie County leaked fracturing fluid and oil).

[55] U.S. Envtl. Prot. Agency, External Review Draft, Assessment of the Potential Impacts of Hydraulic Fracturing for Oil and Gas on Drinking Water Resources at 5–42 (June 2015), *available at* http://cfpub.epa.gov/ncea/hfstudy/recordisplay.cfm?deid=244651.

[56] *Id.* at 5–48.

[57] *See, e.g.*, Williams Cty., N.D., Well Name Dave Arnson 8–5 1–H, Incident 20110613213356 (May 31, 2011), http://www.ndhealth.gov/EHS/FOIA/Spills/Summary_Reports/20110613213356_Summary_Report.pdf ("2 bbls of flowback fluid ran off the edge of wellsite for approximately 100 ft."; berm constructed, contaminants vacuumed; potential environmental risk of soil contamination but no water body affected); Mountrail Cty., N.D., Well Name Crowfoot 35–3031H, Incident 20110112143928 (Jan. 11, 2011), http://www.ndhealth.gov/EHS/FOIA/Spills/Summary_Reports/20110112143928_Summary_Report.pdf (release of 120 barrels of flowback from a truck to a well site; 50 barrels recovered); Greene Cty., Pa., API Permit 059–25160, Enforcement ID 250351 (Sept. 23, 2009), http://www.depreportingservices.state.pa.us/ReportServer/Pages/ReportViewer.aspx?/Oil_Gas/OG_Compliance (flowback released into field from pit; haul trucks responded); San Juan Cty., N.M., API 30–045–29969, Incident nJK1217341013 (May 17, 2000), https://www.apps.emnrd.state.nm.us/ocd/ocdpermitting/Data/Incidents/SpillSearchResultsExcel.aspx?Api=30-045-29969 (noting 100 barrels of flowback that spilled; no barrels recovered).

the EPA, flowback and produced water have polluted groundwater.[58] Some fractured wells also have deficient or defective underground casing and cement,[59] and inspectors have detected methane coming out of these wells at the surface.[60]

The HF Rule addresses these and other externalities of oil and gas drilling and fracturing. By requiring data such as the geology where wells will be drilled and fractured, existing natural faults and fractures, old wellbores near the proposed well, nearby sources of usable water, and the proposed depth of the well and fractures,[61] the BLM will better understand (and be able to manage) how the drilling and fracturing of a well could potentially cause the leakage of methane or other substances into nearby faults or old wells—leakage that could potentially allow substances to migrate to the surface and impact surface water and soil in addition to underground resources.[62] By requiring monitoring of cementing operations, the preparation of cement evaluation logs where cement does not reach the surface of the well, and remedial action where it appears that cement is inadequate,[63] the HF Rule helps to ensure that wells—which will be subjected to high pressures as a result of hydraulic fracturing—will not leak, again helping to prevent the possible contamination of underground and surface resources. The portions of the HF Rule addressing the casing and cementing of wells also help to ensure that gas and oil will not escape wells and that water will not mix with oil and gas,[64] thus preventing the waste of valuable Federal resources and money earned from those resources. Further, by requiring the disclosure of chemicals used in fracturing,[65] the BLM helps to inform the public, including other users of public lands, of the chemicals that are stored on site and contained in the flowback. And the BLM achieves multiple environmental goals, including operator compliance with the Migratory Bird Treaty Act,[66] Bald and Golden Eagle Protection Act,[67] Clean Water Act (CWA),[68] and Resource Conservation and Recovery Act (RCRA),[69] by requiring tank storage of flowback.[70]

Furthermore, in balancing the importance of oil and gas development with other values on Federal lands, including environmental protection, the rule is not overly

---

[58] Envtl. Prot. Agency, Assessment of the Potential Impacts, *supra* note 55, at 7–36 to 7–37.

[59] *See, e.g.*, Bradford Cty., Pa., API Permit 015–21704, Violation ID 645597 (Aug. 2, 2012), http://www.depreportingservices.state.pa.us/ReportServer/Pages/ReportViewer.aspx?/Oil_Gas/OG_Compliance (noting that "[w]ell has been fraced" and indicating a "[f]ailure to report defective, insufficient, or improperly cemented casing").

[60] All of the following examples of incidents are from Pennsylvania records of unconventional wells at which inspectors from the Commonwealth took enforcement action. *See* Pa. Dept. of Envtl. Prot., Oil and Gas Compliance Report, http://www.depreportingservices.state.pa.us/ReportServer/Pages/ReportViewer.aspx?/Oil_Gas/OG_Compliance (select "Inspections With Violations Only" and "Unconventional Only"). Unconventional wells are those that "generally cannot be produced except by horizontal or vertical wellbores stimulated by hydraulic fracturing." Pa. Dept. of Envtl. Prot., Report Instructions for the *Oil and Gas Compliance Report* at 5, http://files.dep.state.pa.us/OilGas/BOGM/BOGMPortalFiles/OilGasReports/HelpDocs/OG_Compliance_Help.pdf. All violations are from http://www.depreportingservices.state.pa.us/ReportServer/Pages/ReportViewer.aspx?/Oil_Gas/OG_Compliance. Lycoming Cty., Pa., API Permit 081–20238, Enforcement ID 268004, Feb. 18, 2011 ("02/14/11 gas bubbling in the cellar found to be in the annular space of the 9⅝ × 13⅜ casing"); Bradford Cty., Pa., API Permit 015–20932, Enforcement ID 288538, Sept. 11, 2012 ("initial complaint water well shows methane levels increased from non-detect to 82.7 mg/L"; "Chesapeake caused or allowed gas from lower formations to enter fresh groundwater"); Clearfield Cty., Pa., API Permit 033–26855, Enforcement ID 265809, Dec. 6, 2010 ("Methane migrated to surface through cement in 9⅝" annulus."). Peer-reviewed sources have estimated rates of well failure for all Marcellus wells to be 2.58%, 3.4%, or 6.2%. *See* Richard J. Davies, Sam Almond, Robert S. Ward, Robert B. Jackson, Charlotte Adams, Fred Worrall, Liam G. Herringshaw, Jon G. Gluyas & Mark A. Whitehead, *Oil and Gas Wells and Their Integrity: Implications for Shale and Unconventional Resource Exploitation*, 16 Marine and Petroleum Geology 239, 243 (2014) (comparing the estimates from peer-reviewed publications).

[61] Oil and Gas; Hydraulic Fracturing on Federal and Indian Lands, *supra* note 2, at 16,218–16,219.

[62] *See* Davies, *supra* note 60, at 240.

[63] Oil and Gas; Hydraulic Fracturing on Federal and Indian Lands, *supra* note 2, at 16,219–16,220.

[64] *See* Ground Water Protection Council, State Oil and Natural Gas Regulations Designed to Protect Water Resources at 12, 19 (2009), http://www.gwpc.org/sites/default/files/state_oil_and_gas_regulations_designed_to_protect_water_resources_0.pdf (prepared for the U.S. Dept. of Energy) (noting early state well casing regulations that prevented water incursion into the well).

[65] Oil and Gas; Hydraulic Fracturing on Federal and Indian Lands, *supra* note 2, at 16,220–16,221.

[66] 16 U.S.C. §§ 703, 707 (2012).

[67] *Id.* at § 668.

[68] 40 C.F.R. §§ 435.50, 435.52 (2013).

[69] 42 U.S.C. § 6945 (2012).

[70] Oil and Gas; Hydraulic Fracturing on Federal and Indian Lands, *supra* note 2, at 16,220.

onerous. As discussed in Part V, some states already require cementing tests that are more stringent than BLM rules. Further, many oil and gas operators already report a range of well data including fracturing chemicals used through FracFocus,[71] and some oil and gas operators already use tanks. For example, Encana reports: "In most of our operations, we use closed-loop fluid handling systems. . . . Because drilling and fracturing fluids do not come into contact with the ground surface, there is less likelihood of groundwater contamination."[72]

IV. NO FEDERAL ENVIRONMENTAL STATUTES PRECLUDE OR DISPLACE THE HF RULE

In addition to having strong support in FLPMA and the MLA, the HF Rule is not precluded or displaced by other Federal statutes that apply to, or exempt, some oil and gas activities from certain Federal environmental regulations. The BLM has long regulated the casing and cementing of wells on Federal lands,[73] among other regulations, and other Federal statutes have not precluded these regulations—nor do these statutes now preclude the updated regulations. The relevant Federal environmental statutes that apply to certain aspects of oil and gas development and fracturing are, *inter alia*, the Safe Drinking Water Act (SDWA), RCRA, the CWA, and the Emergency Planning and Community Right-to-Know Act (EPCRA). The SDWA applies to certain entities that inject substances underground and requires those entities to obtain a permit that ensures that injection will not endanger underground sources of drinking water.[74] The Act exempts from the definition of "injection" any hydraulic fracturing that is done without the use of diesel.[75] The EPA also exempts most oil and gas exploration and production (E&P) wastes from Subtitle C of RCRA—a subtitle that requires cradle-to-grave tracking of the generation, transport, and disposal of hazardous wastes and sets standards for transport and disposal.[76] Under the CWA, the EPA prohibits certain discharges of oil and gas wastes into surface waters[77] and has proposed to prohibit discharge of flowback from unconventional wells to certain wastewater treatment plants.[78] Finally, the EPCRA requires hydraulic fracturing operators to keep records of hazardous substances that are stored on site[79] but does not require these operators to annually report releases of these substances.[80]

The HF Rule does not conflict with any of these Federal rules or exemptions. The rule is not precluded by other Federal statutes and exemptions for three reasons. First, Congress includes limited, individual oil and gas exemptions in statutes that address different types of pollution and that are administered by different agencies. In providing these exemptions, Congress has not indicated an intent to preclude regulation by different agencies under different statutes. Second, environmental statutes are commonly structured to include discrete exemptions: Congress often exempts an activity from a statute knowing that the activity is or might be regulated under a different statute. Third, the purpose of the environmental statutes in question is primarily to limit the environmental externalities of certain private entity and local government activities without unduly limiting the productive use of private property; it is not to limit a Federal agency's authority to manage *federally-owned and federally-managed* land in a manner consistent with its statutory mandate.

---

[71] FracFocus Chemical Disclosure Registry, http://fracfocus.org/ (showing 99,734 sites registered as of July 12, 2015); Keith B. Hall, *Hydraulic Fracturing: Trade Secrets and the Mandatory Disclosure of Fracturing Water Composition*, 49 Idaho L. Rev. 399 (2013) (describing state disclosure requirements).

[72] Encana®, Fluid storage, disposal and reuse, https://www.encana.com/sustainability/environment/water/fracturing/fluid-storage.html (last visited July 10, 2015).

[73] *See* Onshore Oil and Gas Order No. 1, *supra* note 24, at § III.D.3 (requiring, *inter alia*, drilling plans including plans for protecting usable water and minerals, blowout prevention plans, and cementing plans); *id.* at § III.F.3 (showing that in approving APDs BLM must attach "conditions of approval" that reflect necessary mitigation, allowing mitigation measures to minimize adverse impacts, and allowing the BLM to require Best Management Practices).

[74] 42 U.S.C. § 300h(b)(1) (2012).

[75] *Id.* at § 300h(d)(1).

[76] Regulatory Determination for Oil and Gas and Geothermal Exploration, Development and Production Wastes, 53 Fed. Reg. 25,446–01 (July 6, 1988).

[77] 40 C.F.R. §§ 435.30. 435.32, 435.50, 435.52 (2013).

[78] Effluent Limitations Guidelines and Standards for the Oil and Gas Extraction Point Source Category, 80 Fed. Reg. 18557 (proposed Apr. 7, 2015).

[79] 42 U.S.C. §§ 11021–11022 (2012).

[80] 42 U.S.C. § 11023(b) (2012); 40 C.F.R. § 372.23 (2013).

A. *Existing Federal environmental statutes indicate no Congressional intent to exempt hydraulic fracturing, casing and cementing, or waste storage from BLM rules. Exemptions under various generally applicable environmental statutes do not exempt hydraulic fracturing activities from all Federal regulation of federally-managed land*

The question of whether one Federal statute precludes the application of another (such as whether the SDWA precludes BLM regulation of oil and gas development and fracturing under FLPMA and the MLA) is one of congressional intent,[81] to be ascertained through statutory interpretation.[82] It is certainly within Congress's power to exempt hydraulic fracturing from all Federal regulation; to date, however, it has (wisely) not chosen to do so,[83] and such a blanket exemption cannot be manufactured from the limited exemptions already in place. An exemption of an industrial activity from one Federal environmental statute does not immunize that activity from other Federal environmental statutes unless the statutory language clearly shows Congressional intent for such immunity.[84] Indeed, an exemption or partial exemption from one statute may promote effective regulation under another statute, thus making the laws complements.[85] The Federal laws that partially apply to the subject matter of the BLM hydraulic fracturing rules, or that exempt hydraulic fracturing from certain aspects of Federal law, do not show any intent to block Federal agencies like BLM from regulating to accomplish their specific statutory mission.

In exempting hydraulic fracturing from the definition of "injection" under the SDWA, the Energy Policy Act of 2005 amends the SDWA to read as follows: "*For purposes of this part:* (1) Underground injection . . . (B) excludes— . . . (ii) the underground injection of fluids or propping agents (other than diesel fuels) pursuant to hydraulic fracturing operations related to oil, gas, or geothermal production activities."[86] The Act simply makes clear that under the SDWA hydraulic fracturing is not an injection activity that must be permitted by the EPA or states. It does not address how fracturing may or should be regulated under other acts or by other agencies. Furthermore, the SDWA's legislative history shows that Congress did not "intend any of the provisions of this bill to repeal or limit any authority," of the U.S. Survey Geological Survey (USGS), one of the BLM's predecessors in regulating Federal oil and gas wells.[87]

The SDWA is inapplicable to both drilling and fracturing of oil and gas production wells; it does not apply to the injection of substances like drilling muds and fluids and fracturing fluids underground, as these activities do not count as injection pursuant to the provision in the Energy Policy Act of 2005 and other provisions.[88] But states and Federal agencies regulating oil and gas drilling and fracturing have other ways to ensure the safety of these practices. Therefore, many other acts, which I

[81] *Felt v. Atchison*, Topeka, and Santa Fe Railroad Co., 60 F.3d 1416, 1419 (9th Cir. 1995).

[82] *POM Wonderful LLC v. The Coca-Cola Company*, 134 S.Ct. 2228, 2236 (2014).

[83] In their briefs opposing the BLM rule, petitioners quote one of my statements out of context. *See* Motion for Preliminary Injunction (Wyoming and Colorado) at 10, *Wyoming v. U.S. Dept. of the Interior*, No. 15–CV–00043–SWS (D. Wyo. May 29, 2015); Hannah Wiseman, *Untested Waters: The Rise of Hydraulic Fracturing in Oil and Gas Production and the Need to Revisit Regulation*, 20 Fordham Envtl. L. Rev. 115, 145 (2009)) (noting that "the Act conclusively withdrew fracing from the realm of Federal regulation" to indicate that Congress exempted hydraulic fracturing from the SDWA, but not to suggest that many other well development stages associated with fracturing, such as flowback disposal and discharge, are exempt from Federal laws). Notably, my article also does not address the separate authority of the BLM to regulate fracturing on Federal lands.

[84] *Cf. POM Wonderful*, 134 S.Ct. at 2236–2237 (in a case interpreting two Federal food labeling statutes, refusing to adopt either a test that would require that full effect be given to each statute and only bar the application of one statute if there is irreconcilable conflict, or a test that would "reconcile" the laws by finding that one law narrows the other, but finding that even under the "reconciliation" test, the best result in the case was not to bar the application of a portion of one statute).

[85] *Cf. POM Wonderful*, 134 S.Ct at 2238 ("When two statutes complement each other, it would show disregard for the congressional design to hold that Congress nonetheless intended one Federal statute to preclude the operation of the other.").

[86] 42 U.S.C. § 300h(d)(1) (2012) (emphasis added).

[87] H.R. Rep. No. 93–1185 at 32 (1974), *as reprinted in* 1974 U.S.C.C.A.N. 6454, 6494.

[88] States have argued that the SDWA is the only Act under which the injection of substances may be regulated based on one line from a Federal case. That case states, "[I]t is clear that Congress dictated that all underground injection be regulated under the [SDWA]." *Legal Envtl. Assistance Found., Inc. v. U.S. Envtl. Protection Agency*, 118 F.3d 1467, 1474 (11th Cir. 1997). This statement does not indicate that only the SDWA may regulate underground injection. Rather, it indicates that all underground injection activities are subject to the SDWA. The case does not address whether underground injection activities might also be subject to other Federal acts, particularly when injection occurs on Federal lands.

introduce above, address drilling, casing, and cementing of wells to ensure that substances do not leak underground and pollute surface and underground water. Many states regulate the casing and cementing of both fractured and conventional oil and gas wells—not under delegated SDWA authority, but rather under their independent regulatory authority to protect the public health, safety, and welfare.[89] Similarly, the BLM may regulate the casing of fractured and conventional wells to fulfill its MLA and FLPMA responsibilities, and, as indicated above, it has long regulated the casing of conventional wells and well stimulation.[90]

Additionally, the SDWA applies to the protection of drinking water and potentially usable water.[91] The Act indicates no intent to regulate fracturing and the cementing and casing of oil and gas wells for the purpose of preventing oil and gas waste and protecting soil and other surface resources, or wildlife. The BLM's rules for the casing and cementing of wells help to achieve all of these results.

Similarly, in exempting certain oil and gas E&P wastes from RCRA in 1988, the EPA indicated no intent to preclude regulation of these wastes under other acts, such as BLM's requirement under the HF Rule that flowback be stored in tanks. Indeed, the EPA indicated that it would rely on other acts like the SDWA (which applies to the disposal of liquid wastes from oil and gas wells, including fractured wells), the CWA, and subtitle D of RCRA, to help improve waste management.[92] Nor did the EPA in the RCRA exemption indicate an intent to prevent other entities from regulating these wastes under other Acts.[93]

With respect to the CWA, the EPA regulates oil and gas waste rather than exempting it, and the HF Rule and other BLM rules help operators comply with CWA rules, such as limits on flowback and produced water discharges.[94] Finally, with respect to chemical disclosure, the EPCRA already requires the maintenance of material safety data sheets for fracturing chemicals at oil and gas sites (with certain trade secret exemptions)[95] and does not indicate an intent to preclude other disclosure regulations implemented by other Federal agencies.

B. Federal environmental statutes are structured in a manner that anticipates that activities will be regulated under certain statutes and exempted from others

The argument that an exemption of an activity from one environmental statute exempts it from similar protections under other statutes administered by other agencies cuts against the very purpose of having varied Federal statutes that address discrete issues, as implemented by various agencies with various missions. For example, some discharges of waste do not count as "solid waste" under RCRA, which regulates the generation, transport, and disposal of waste, because these discharges are instead regulated under the CWA.[96] Indeed, certain environmental statutes contain an explicit "anti-duplication" provision; in one case a Federal district court noted that the "the pollution discharges at issue in this case are exempted from the coverage of the Recovery Act because they are instead regulated by the Clean Water Act."[97] In the oil and gas context, despite the RCRA subtitle C exemption for oil and gas E&P wastes,[98] an oil and gas operator that causes contamination of land with certain oil and gas E&P wastes is liable for the costs of clean-up under the Comprehensive Environmental Response, Compensation, and Liability Act.[99] And if the BLM is concerned that management of these wastes would contaminate these public lands and prevent their future productive use for grazing or other purposes (and generate CERCLA liability), it may regulate the management of these wastes under its FLPMA and MLA responsibilities.

---

[89] See Ground Water Protection Council, supra note 64; Wiseman, Risk and Response, supra note 49 (describing state casing and cementing regulations).

[90] See supra note 24.

[91] See, e.g., H.R. Rep. No. 93–1185, supra note 87, at 1 ("The purpose of the legislation is to assure that water supply systems serving the public meet minimum national standards for protection of public health.").

[92] Regulatory Determination, supra note 76, at 25,456.

[93] The EPA indicated that it would help the states improve their oil and gas waste regulations. Regulatory Determination, supra note 76, at 25,456. As discussed in Part IV of this testimony, state oil and gas regulations still vary and might leave gaps.

[94] 40 C.F.R. §§ 435.50, 435.52 (2013).

[95] 2 U.S.C. §§ 11021–11022 (2012); 29 C.F.R. § 1910.1200(i) (2013).

[96] 42 U.S.C. § 6903(27) (2012); see also Sheldon M. Novick & Donald W. Stever, Envtl. L. Inst., 2 Law of Environmental Protection § 14:32 (2015) (discussing this exemption and noting that "[t]he boundaries between RCRA and other statutes are marked by a series of exclusions from the definition of 'hazardous waste.'").

[97] Jones v. E.R. Snell Contractor, Inc., 333 F.Supp.2d 1344, 1350 (N.D. Ga. 2004).

[98] Regulatory Determination, supra note 92.

[99] 42 U.S.C. § 9607(a) (2012).

C. Federal environmental statutes aim primarily at private actors and do not comprehensively address the unique responsibilities of Federal agencies to protect public natural resources

The CWA, SDWA, Clean Air Act, and other Federal environmental statutes primarily address the many corporations and other entities that engage in profitable activity while also producing externalities in the form of pollution. These acts were not designed with the primary intent of addressing additional responsibilities of Federal agencies managing activities that occur on *public* lands—lands that the agencies must manage for multiple uses for current and future generations. There are, as a result, numerous examples of activities that are exempt from at least one Federal environmental statute but are regulated by the BLM. For example, the CWA exempts soil runoff from certain agricultural and timber harvesting operations from certain CWA requirements administered by the Environmental Protection Agency and states.[100] However, the BLM regulates soil runoff from farming, ranching, or certain timber harvesting to protect waters and federally-protected endangered species in those waters.[101] Indeed, a failure of the BLM to regulate the environmental impacts of these activities might violate Congressional directives for the agency, which require, *inter alia*, regulation of land use to protect environmental resources.[102] Similarly, a failure of the BLM to regulate the environmental impacts of oil and gas extraction on public lands, simply because certain aspects of oil and gas extraction are exempt from the SDWA, RCRA, and other Federal acts, would be an abdication of the BLM's statutorily defined responsibilities on public lands.

V. THE HF RULE DOES NOT DUPLICATE STATE REGULATIONS AND WILL AUGMENT STATE REGULATION AND ENFORCEMENT IN USEFUL WAYS

In addition to providing important environmental protection and following statutorily defined duties to enable multi-use development of public lands, the HF Rule beneficially augments state regulation of oil and gas development, including fracturing. The rule provides an important overlay above various (and variable) state requirements. The portions of the HF Rule that are not more stringent than existing state and tribal regulations will likely not require variances[103] because BLM rules already serve as a floor, not a ceiling, to state rules.[104] And the HF Rule portions that are more stringent than state regulations protect important Federal values without imposing a one-size-fits-all approach. For example, if the BLM determines that well integrity was compromised during fracturing or that cement in the well was inadequate, a remediation strategy will be formed on a case-by-case basis.[105]

Several portions of the BLM rule demonstrate how the rule is more stringent than certain state requirements and less stringent than others, thus revealing the variability of state regulations that currently apply to oil and gas operations. For example, Colorado requires operators to run a cement bond log—a specific type of cement evaluation log—when operators use certain types of casing,[106] and New Mexico requires these logs in some counties.[107] Other states do not require these logs.[108] But in states where evaluation logs have been required, oil and gas development

---

[100] *See* 33 U.S.C. § 1342(l) (2012) (exempting from the Clean Water Act National Pollutant Discharge Elimination System permitting requirement "silviculture activities," including "harvesting operations," and "agricultural return flows"); 33 U.S.C. § 1362(14) (2012) (exempting from the definition of a "point source" of pollution "agricultural stormwater discharges and return flows from irrigated agriculture"). These sources are regulated as nonpoint sources, particularly where a total maximum daily load has been established for a water into which the sources discharge.

[101] *See, e.g.*, Bureau of Land Mgmt., U.S. Dep't. of the Interior, Draft Resource Management Plan/Environmental Impact Statement: Western Oregon at 3–908 (2015), *available at*, http://www.blm.gov/or/plans/rmpswesternoregon/files/draft/RMP_EIS_Volume3.pdf (in management directions for forested lands and timber harvesting, prohibiting mechanical treatments on "steep slopes" or "sensitive soils" to protect "[p]erennial and fish-bearing streams").

[102] *See supra* Part II of this testimony.

[103] Oil and Gas; Hydraulic Fracturing on Federal and Indian Lands, *supra* note 2, at 16,221.

[104] Second Declaration of Steven Wells ¶ 22, *Wyoming v. U.S. Dept. of the Interior*, No. 2:15–CV–43–SWS (D. Wyo. June 12, 2015).

[105] Oil and Gas; Hydraulic Fracturing on Federal and Indian Lands, *supra* note 2, at 16,219–16,220.

[106] 2 Colo. Code Regs. § 404–1:317(p) (2015).

[107] N.M. Admin. Code R, §§ 19.15.39.8, 19.15.39.9 (2015).

[108] For example, Utah requires well completion or recompletion reports but does not appear to require a specific cement evaluation log. Utah Admin Code R. § 649–3–21 (2015). It appears that Wyoming only requires a description of the cementing program. Wyo. Rules and Regs., Oil Gen. Ch. 3 § 8(c)(8).

does not appear to have been inhibited.[109] Thus, the HF Rule provides a consistent requirement for fracturing on Federal lands without imposing an unduly burdensome requirement.

In another example of a portion of the HF Rule that is equally as stringent as certain state regulations and more stringent than others, the rule (as discussed above) generally requires the use of tanks for the storage of flowback,[110] subject to certain exceptions. Colorado requires operators to use tanks for drilling and/or fracturing within a certain number of feet of a public water system,[111] and New Mexico allows pits but requires operators using pits to obtain a permit and to follow specific siting, construction, and operational guidelines for pits or tanks.[112] Although Utah does not appear to require tanks for flowback, the state requires oil and gas operators to "[m]aintain [flowback] tanks in a workmanlike manner that will preclude leakage and provide for all applicable safety measures . . . ."[113]

To the extent that portions of the HF Rule duplicate state or tribal requirements, operators have several options. A variance may be granted (or may be unnecessary) if the state or tribal rule meets or exceeds the objectives of BLM regulation. Further, because most of the HF Rule requirements are informational—requiring information about geology, fracturing chemicals used, and cement evaluation logs prepared, for example—operators can meet any duplicative state requirements by submitting the same information to the BLM and to the state or tribe.[114] Indeed, the HF Rule requires much of the information to be submitted through the Web site FracFocus, just as many states do. By inputting information into FracFocus, the operator will comply simultaneously with certain state, tribal, and Federal requirements.

Just as the HF Rule provides consistent requirements for drilling and fracturing on Federal lands above varied state requirements, the BLM's enforcement resources can help complement what are often limited state enforcement resources. In a number of states, inspectors have done an admirable job of visiting more well sites and noting potential violations of state laws at these sites in the midst of a drilling and fracturing boom. But state resources are limited, in part due to funding limitations. For example, in 2012 Colorado had approximately 36 oil and gas inspectors and 49,062 active conventional and unconventional oil and gas wells, whereas New Mexico had approximately 12 inspectors for 56,366 active conventional and unconventional wells.[115] The most important inspections occur during the drilling, completion, and fracturing of the well, and a far smaller number of wells are drilled, fractured, and completed each day than the total number of active wells listed. But active, producing wells, too, can cause environmental problems, such as leaking oil, condensate, or produced water from tanks[116] or from on-site equipment that does minimal processing.[117] Thus, inspectors' time must be split between wells being drilled, completed, and fractured and those under production, and enforcement resources are often thin. States often fund oil and gas enforcement programs through permitting fees and other fees, and where these fees are statutorily prescribed, they have in some cases not been adjusted for inflation for many years.[118] As a result of these and other state deficiencies, "[e]nforcement rates for spills and other shale gas waste pollution incidents are low, and the punishment may not be deterring risky behavior."[119]

---

[109] For natural gas wells alone, in 2014 Colorado had 32,371 producing gas wells, and New Mexico had 27,957 producing gas wells. Energy Info. Admin., Number of Producing Gas Wells, http://www.eia.gov/dnav/ng/ng_prod_wells_s1_a.htm (last visited July 5, 2015).

[110] Oil and Gas; Hydraulic Fracturing on Federal and Indian Lands, *supra* note 2, at 16,220.

[111] 2 Colo. Code Regs. § 404–1:317B (2015).

[112] N.M Admin. Code R. § 19.15.17.9 (2015).

[113] Utah Admin Code R. § 649–3.1.2.4 (2015).

[114] For example, Wyoming (like the BLM in its HF Rule) requires information on the geologic formation into which well stimulation fluids will be injected, well stimulation design including anticipated pressures, the base fluid for fracturing, and chemicals used in fracturing. Wyo. Rules and Regs., Oil Gen. Ch. 3 § 45(c)–(e) (2015).

[115] Hannah Wiseman, *Regulatory Risks in Tight Oil and Gas Development*, 29 Nat. Gas & Electricity 6 (2012).

[116] Envtl. Protection Agency, Assessment of the Potential Impacts, *supra* note 55, at 7–31 through 7–36.

[117] *See, e.g.,* Bradford Cty., Pa., API Permit 015–20425, Violation ID 600818, Dec. 2, 2010 ("Orange liquid seaping [sic] out from underneath seperator [sic] and heater treater."); Washington Cty., Pa., API Permit 125–22688, Violation ID 619012, June 28, 2011 (noting brine/condensate leak from separator).

[118] *See* Hannah J. Wiseman, *The Capacity of States to Govern Shale Gas Development Risks*, 48 Envtl. Sci. & Tech. 8376, 8384 (2014).

[119] Katherine E. Konschnick & Mark K. Boling, *Shale Gas Development: A Smart Regulation Framework*, 48 Envtl. Sci. & Tech. 8404, 8409 (2014). *See also* Terrence J. Centner & Laura

While the BLM, too, has limited enforcement resources,[120] combining the expertise and resources of the BLM with states can help to ensure that wells on Federal lands are regularly inspected and that violations—which can sometimes result from vandalism, weather, or other issues beyond the direct control of the operator—are quickly and effectively addressed. Between Fiscal Year 2007 and 2012, the BLM increased the number of environmental inspections of wells "by approximately 63 percent" and conducted a total of 17,866 environmental inspections in Fiscal Year 2012.[121]

CONCLUSION

The BLM's HF Rule provides a needed update to Federal oil and gas rules that have not kept up with rapid changes in U.S. oil and gas development. The BLM has long regulated the casing and cementing of wells, storage of oil and gas wastes, and provision of data to Federal authorities to follow its statutory requirements—namely, to ensure that oil and gas development is compatible with other uses of Federal lands for current and future generations and to protect water and environmental resource values, among other values. The HF Rule further achieves these goals. Primarily through informational requirements, the rule informs BLM officials about potential problems with wells, such as wells drilled in areas with old wells—which could pose a risk if fracturing intercepted other wells—and wells that have inadequate cement to secure casing and prevent leakage of substances from and into the well. The rule augments rather than conflicts with other Federal requirements, fulfilling agency-specific mandates that are not contained within other Federal environmental statutes. The HF Rule also complements and improves upon state requirements and provides a variance provision in the event that duplicative informational rules—which could simply require an operator to submit the same report to a state and Federal official—are deemed onerous and unnecessary.

————

Dr. FLEMING. Thank you, Ms. Wiseman. At this point we are going to move along to questions from the dais. We will be recognizing Members for 5 minutes, and I now recognize myself for 5 minutes.

I would like to say in the opening here, that both Secretaries Jewell and Salazar of the Interior have testified that they are not aware of any harm from hydraulic fracturing over the 50 or 60 years of its history to human beings, or contamination of any water supply, which really begs the question in a period of an $18 trillion national debt, why we want to add another layer of regulations for fracturing and horizontal drilling. Mr. Lowenthal suggests that this is just a floor on regulations. But if the floor is all the way up to the ceiling, then that really doesn't give operators much room to move.

My first question is to Director Kornze. As you know, the state of Louisiana has been effectively regulating hydraulic fracturing for some time. It has been claimed that the BLM will grant states a variance if their regulation meets or exceeds the Federal rule. Does that mean that you would delegate authority to the state to regulate on behalf of the Federal Government?

Mr. KORNZE. Chairman, I appreciate the question. We have authorities to regulate on public lands. Those are found in the Federal Land Policy and Management Act, in the Mineral Leasing

Kathryn O'Connell, *Unfinished Business in the Regulation of Shale Gas Production in the United States*, 476–477 Sci. Total Env't. 359, 364 (2014) (noting that "some governments are placed in an uncomfortable position of having laws and regulations to protect people but an inadequate infrastructure for the enforcement of the requirements").

[120] U.S. Govt. Accountability Office, Oil and Gas Development, GAO–13–572, BLM Needs Better Data to Track Permit Processing Times and Prioritize Inspections (2013), *available at* http://www.gao.gov/assets/660/657176.pdf.

[121] *Id.* at 30.

Act, and the Indian Mineral Leasing statutes. We use those to set forth our standards, and we have a very long history of working with states in a cooperative manner to make sure that oil and gas regulation works on the ground. So we have that history in Louisiana, we have that history in all the states present here that——

Dr. FLEMING. But would you be delegating that authority to the state in that instance?

Mr. KORNZE. In my opening statement, I mentioned that there will be areas that are central to the litigation in question that I won't be able to go into. This is one of those central questions about authority delegation. So, I am going to have to politely decline to get into that question deeply, but I——

Dr. FLEMING. So you decline to answer. You are saying that BLM will duplicate the work of the state in requiring to see all the same documents, approve the same permits, and accomplish the same regulatory enforcement. In other words, we would have duplication of effort. You, or whoever is regulating this on the Federal level, would be essentially reviewing the same documents, the same process that the state would, simultaneously.

Mr. KORNZE. Well, I think it is important to clarify that we have a very long history, which I think the professor did an excellent job of laying out——

Dr. FLEMING. Well, before you go into all that detail, just give me a yes or a no on that, please.

Mr. KORNZE. Well, I think it is essential to talk about the fact that we have——

Dr. FLEMING. Let's start with a yes or no answer. Would you be duplicating efforts?

Mr. KORNZE. I don't believe there is duplication, because there is no fundamental change from this rule, in terms of how this relationship works. Since the Mineral Leasing Act in 1920, the Federal Government has stepped forward and had this rule that we have today——

Dr. FLEMING. Well, let's fast-forward to today. Have there been any variances granted to date?

Mr. KORNZE. We have not signed any formal documents related to variances, but we have had some very productive conversations with states, and have identified places where we do think that variances would be available.

Dr. FLEMING. So, no variance would be granted while the litigation is pending. Is that correct?

Mr. KORNZE. The judge has requested that we not implement the rule, that he has postponed the enforcement date. So, as part of that, we have stood down on the——

Dr. FLEMING. Even in the cases of the states that are not affected, you would not grant variances in those states either?

Mr. KORNZE. "Not affected"? What does that mean?

Dr. FLEMING. Well, those states that aren't involved in the lawsuit, the litigation itself.

Mr. KORNZE. Yes, the judge's order, to my understanding, applies to the rule everywhere.

Dr. FLEMING. OK. Now, I would like to turn to how this rule directly affects my district in Louisiana. In my district there are certain areas of split estate ownership. I am running low on time, so I will try to abbreviate this a bit. Basically, we may have instances where drilling, particularly horizontal drilling, may interface with both multiple private property owners and the Federal Government.

How does this rule—how do we deal with this, when we have a hodge-podge, if you will, of private owners, private mineral interests, as well as on private land, with Federal land? And in some cases it may be Federal land with private ownership of the minerals themselves.

Mr. KORNZE. So the way that it works, Chairman—and I appreciate the question—is that if your wellbore penetrates Federal minerals, then this rule applies.

Dr. FLEMING. All right, very good. Thank you. The Chair now recognizes the Ranking Member for 5 minutes.

Mr. LOWENTHAL. Thank you.

Ms. Wiseman, the states of Colorado and Wyoming use a line from one of your articles to support their argument that the Halliburton loophole in the 2005 Energy Policy Act was intended to keep the Federal Government out of fracking regulations entirely. Do you agree with that?

Ms. WISEMAN. I do not agree with that statement. With due respect to the states, I believe that they quote my article out of context. The article explores the history of the exemption of hydraulic fracturing from the Safe Drinking Water Act and the activities leading up to that exemption, and it focuses only on the Safe Drinking Water Act. The article concludes that, under the Safe Drinking Water Act, Congress clearly and expressly exempted the regulation of hydraulic fracturing, with the exception of diesel fuel, from the Safe Drinking Water Act.

But the article goes on to discuss the other ways in which other Federal laws could potentially still apply to hydraulic fracturing, and have applied to hydraulic fracturing. The article also does not address the authority of Federal agencies to regulate hydraulic fracturing on Federal lands.

Mr. LOWENTHAL. Thank you. I would also like to point out that these same states quote two Members of Congress from 2005 to support their argument. Then it was Congressman Markey and Senator Feingold. We contacted now-Senator Markey—it was Congressman Markey at the time—we contacted Senator Markey about this, and he said, and I quote, "Congress didn't write a get-out-of-any-regulation-forever-free card for fracking. Any attempt to extract any other reading out of the Congressional Record clearly fractures credulity."

Director Kornze and Professor Wiseman, the Chairman of this Full Committee said recently, and I quote, "The DOE and the EPA have both found fracturing safe." Factcheck.org has already pointed out this is not what the EPA found. But could either of you clarify what the Department of Energy has said?

Ms. WISEMAN. The Department of Energy, in its Shale Gas Production Subcommittee report, notes a need to improve certain aspects of the regulation of fracturing, including concerns about hydraulic fracturing with diesel fuel, and concerns about the integrity of well casing.

With respect to the Environmental Protection Agency, page 6–15 of the Environmental Protection Agency Water Quality Study, in one example, points to an incident in Dunn County, North Dakota, when the production surface and conductor casing of a particular well ruptured, and sampling of two monitoring wells in the drinking water aquifer identified brine contamination and tert-Butyl alcohol that was potentially a product of the hydraulic fracturing fluid. That is just one example from the Environmental Protection Agency report.

Mr. LOWENTHAL. Thank you. I am going to move on to Director Kornze. It seems to me that the Republican argument starts with the conclusion that this rule being astronomically expensive, it is going to impose crushing operational administrative burdens on oil and gas drillers. Your agency says that is not the case. I would like to know how you came up with your estimates, and I want you to answer, did you just make these estimates up to make the rule look more affordable?

Mr. KORNZE. Ranking Member, I appreciate the question. We have a team of very accomplished economists that look at publicly available information, that work with our engineers in the field, and use our knowledge from the ground, that look at publications from journals, that take information from the Energy Information Administration, that look at API documents. These are professional documents that are put together, with some significant effort and significant review, including at the Office of Management and Budget, where economists look at them over there. So we feel very good about the product that we have put forward.

Mr. LOWENTHAL. Thank you. Again, Director Kornze, this is my last question for this—we have heard here, and my colleague from Wyoming is very proud of the strong fracking rules her state has implemented. There is concern that once the BLM rule goes into effect, these strong rules would be overturned. I could certainly understand her concern if that was the case.

But let's say your rule went into effect tomorrow, the litigation was completed. Would a company drilling on Federal land in Wyoming need to stop doing those things that the state requires, in order to come into compliance with the BLM rule?

Mr. KORNZE. If the company is complying with the BLM rule and the Wyoming rule, they are good to go.

Mr. LOWENTHAL. So it would be required to comply with the—as long as it complied with the BLM, the floor, it would be required, in Wyoming, to also comply with the Wyoming rule. Is that not true?

Mr. KORNZE. As long as they are meeting the floor, they are good.

Mr. LOWENTHAL. Thank you, and I yield back.

Dr. FLEMING. The gentleman yields back. Dr. Gosar is recognized for 5 minutes.

Dr. GOSAR. Thank you very much.

Councilmember Olguin, you testify, and I quote, "Notwithstanding our requests and suggestions, BLM proceeded to develop draft proposed regulations in isolation and without disclosing its activities to the tribes." Do you believe that one of the main reasons BLM's final fracking rule is so flawed is because the agency didn't adequately consult with the tribes to involve them in this rulemaking?

Mr. OLGUIN. Yes, I do. And the reason I say that, if I may, is being involved in the initial consultation, it was more of an invitation to come and listen to what the rulemaking was all about. However, it wasn't until later on that the actual true spirit of consultation really became evident, that tribes were being considered. So, yes.

Dr. GOSAR. Director Kornze, why did the BLM not adequately consult the tribes before putting out its over-reaching fracking rule?

Mr. KORNZE. Congressman, we undertook a major consultation effort with hundreds of tribes across the country. We held regional meetings, we held a great number of individual meetings. I personally went out to some of these meetings, including to North Dakota, where there is very heavy oil and gas development, to sit down with tribes. We are always striving to do better in the area of consultation. It is something that is very important to us.

Dr. GOSAR. So how do you address the Councilman right to your left? Are you calling him a liar?

Mr. KORNZE. I don't think we are anywhere near that. My point is that we have——

Dr. GOSAR. No, I am very aware of what the Federal Government does with tribes and what they consider consultation, and it is a far cry from applications that you are putting forth, whether it be from health care to now, with mineral rights. It is despicable.

Councilmember Olguin, BLM proceeded to develop the draft proposal regulations in isolation without disclosing its activities to Tribes—let me skip forward. Then let me restate my question, Director Kornze. Why did the BLM not adequately consult the tribes before putting its over-reaching fracking rules forward?

Mr. KORNZE. So my answer remains the same, that we had a very significant consultation effort nationwide, and on an individual basis, and on a regional basis, and we are always in dialog with tribes. These are important relationships for us. We also made changes in the rule that is clarified in our final draft, in the rule that was promulgated, laying out where those ideas came from, and what changes we made in response to tribal concerns.

Dr. GOSAR. Director Kornze, as you know, the BLM proposed to consolidate its New Mexico and Arizona state offices. Last month, the House Appropriations Committee released the Fiscal Year 2016 Interior and Environmental Appropriations Bill, and included the strong language and accompanying reporting that is stating, and I quote, "The committee directs the Bureau not to consolidate the Arizona and New Mexico state offices, and reminds the Bureau that the office consolidation proposals are subject to the committee's reprogram requirements."

Is your agency still planning to move forward with this proposal merger, or will you adhere to the House Appropriation Committee's direction?

Mr. KORNZE. Congressman, we are still looking at the matter. We are aware of the language. We have heard your concerns loudly, we have also heard concerns from the Ranking Member of the Full Committee. We are taking that all into account.

As we have stated previously, we have a strong priority in pushing resources and positions to our field and district offices where that work takes place. In the last 5 years, we have lost 1,300 employees, positions in the Bureau of Land Management. So we have some large stresses in the organization, and I appreciate the work of this committee and your own commitment to work with us to find ways to strengthen the organization.

So, all those things are being looked at right now, and we will be getting back to you in a formal manner, when the time is right, related to that question.

Dr. GOSAR. Councilmember Olguin, thank you again for being here. At the preliminary injunction hearing, the judge asked a government attorney if he knew what percentage of tribal trust lands would have been—which have no regulation of hydraulic fracturing. "If this rule does not go into effect," the attorney responded, "I don't know, and I don't know if we know."

The attorney further continued that, in order to know such a number, it would require knowledge of many different tribal codes, but that he didn't think that the specific information was gathered. When the judge heard this, he responded that, "You might want to consult with the Ute Tribe some more," to which the attorney responded, "I understand some tribes are a little less happy than others."

Councilmember, do you have any comment on this exchange, particularly in respect of how the attorney stated that some tribes are a little less happy than others?

Mr. OLGUIN. I am not sure I have the answer to that, not being present. If I may have a moment?

Dr. GOSAR. Sure.

Mr. OLGUIN. It has been clarified for me. The tribe that was mentioned in that conversation was the Ute Indian Tribe, which is the tribe out of Utah. We, ourselves, as Southern Utes located in Colorado, we actually developed our own hydraulic fracturing rule, which, in essence, is—we don't agree with it.

Dr. GOSAR. So one last question. Does the variance provision do enough to address your concerns about the final rule? Why or why not?

Mr. OLGUIN. The variance, we are not even going to seek it. And it is really for the reason that we are going to exercise our tribal sovereignty, which is the reason why we passed our own regulation.

Dr. GOSAR. So, if this rule goes into effect as written—oh, I am sorry. I yield back the balance of my time.

Mr. LAMBORN [presiding]. Representative Polis.

Mr. POLIS. I thank the gentleman from Colorado, the great state of the Southern Utes, for the time. My question is to the Councilmember from the Southern Utes, Mr. Olguin.

I want to thank you for being here. Of course, it is critical that Indian Country is a part of these discussions. Tribes, like communities, like counties and cities and states, should have authority to determine whether or not they want to use fracking as an element of their economic development strategy, how they want to use it. That is a discussion across Colorado. Counties and municipalities in my district and across our state are having these discussions, whether fracking is something they want to see on their lands and their jurisdiction, where and how they want to have it—which brings me to an issue that you have been very involved with, Mr. Olguin, the issue of sovereignty and local control.

While my colleagues across the aisle seem to argue for those pillars of democracy at times, they continue to act in support of state preemption when it comes to the ability of a municipality or a county to restrict or ban fracking within its bounds.

My question for you, since you are, of course, a champion of sovereignty for your people and the Southern Utes, I want to get your opinion on the matter. I think that we should allow tribes or states or counties to decide how to implement fracking, whether to have it or not, where to have it, and the rules under which it occurs. And I want to ask whether you agree with that premise, Councilmember, that it should be locally determined, as to how and when and if to implement fracking.

Mr. OLGUIN. Well, as far as me being able to answer that, I can only speak for us, as the Southern Ute Tribe. And, yes, I honestly feel very truly and wholeheartedly that it is up to the Southern Ute Indian Tribal Council to determine what rules it will implement, and how those rules will be carried forward.

Mr. POLIS. So if your council didn't want fracking, you don't think that the Federal or state government should force fracking to occur on your lands. Is that correct?

Mr. OLGUIN. Correct.

Mr. POLIS. And, of course, if you do want fracking, you want to make sure that it is done in the manner under the direction of your council, as opposed to by the Federal or state government. Is that correct?

Mr. OLGUIN. Yes.

Mr. POLIS. OK. That is certainly consistent with my viewpoint. We have, as you know, a problem in Colorado—and different counties and cities have differing opinions. There are some counties that embrace fracking, like Weld County. It is an important part of their economic development strategy. We have other cities, like the city of Fort Collins, which I represent, which has banned fracking, but is being sued to force them to have it, even though they have chosen not to. I think that that would be a dangerous precedent, if that decision goes the wrong way.

I think that for all of us to get along, we need to reflect the diversity of the country. Of course, on the tribal side there will be some tribes that want to embrace fracking, and even those tribes will probably limit the areas it occurs. I would imagine you might have areas that are ancestral holy areas, or burial grounds, where you may not want to have that kind of activity, and you will have other areas where you do. But that should certainly be left up to you, not entities in other areas of the government.

I do want to go to Mr. Kornze, as well. I want to thank Mr. Kornze for being here. We have, of course, some fracking regulations. And many are arguing that fracking is safe. But, according to recently released data, there are health-based rules that are being violated every day with regard to fracking. Between 2011 and 2014, the top 20 offending fracking companies across the state committed an average of 1.5 violations a day. That is just in Pennsylvania.

So, I am not here to argue about whether fracking is safe or not, but I want to talk about a series of bills that Representative Cartwright, DeGette, Schakowsky, and I have introduced, the frack pack, to increase safeguards around fracking and, of course, in the belief that they should be implemented.

Now, that kind of action needs to come from this body. But if you agree with the premise that fracking, to the extent it is done, should be done safely, I want to ask what you can do administratively, above and beyond the rules in question that are being litigated, to ensure that violating companies and decidedly unsafe practices are kept to a minimum.

Mr. KORNZE. Well, thank you, Congressman, for the question— we work closely with industry, state regulators, and many others, to make sure that, one, we have the best practices taking place in the field, and that we are working as a team. And also, that when we see violations, that we are addressing them. So that, in addition to the long history of Federal regulation of oil and gas development on public lands and Indian lands, it is a joint cooperative effort that we do to address the point you raised.

Mr. POLIS. Now, it is my understanding that inspections and compliance are insufficient. Is there anything you can do to beef up inspections to ensure compliance of existing rules?

Mr. KORNZE. At this point, we do have a great need that the Inspector General and the Government Accounting Office have both pointed out. BLM needs to do our job correctly for the 100,000-plus wells that we have oversight responsibility for. We need about 220 inspectors.

Mr. POLIS. How many do you have?

Mr. KORNZE. Right now we have about 160. So we have repeatedly, through the years, put forward a proposal in our budget to get the funding that we need for that part of our program. And I do hope that this year the Congress will grant us that part of our program, so that we can do the job when it comes to oversight.

Mr. POLIS. Thank you. I yield back.

Mr. LAMBORN. OK, thank you. Before I start my questions, let me first say I apologize for not being here earlier. I was in another committee, where we had a critical markup on a piece of legislation that had to go to the Floor, so that is why I was late. But I am so glad that we are having this hearing today. Thank you, Director, for being here, and everyone who is here, including the gentleman from Colorado.

And let me also say that we have had many hearings on this subject while the BLM was working on this proposed regulation. For years, for several Congresses now, we have had a number of hearings. We have had field hearings, like one in Denver at the State Capitol. And here in Washington, we have had a number of hearings. So it is so good that we can continue the scrutiny on this important subject.

With that, I would like to ask Director Kornze a question. The rule that you are working on states that one of the goals of a final rule is to "promote the development of more stringent standards by state and tribal governments." Can you tell the committee specifically which states and tribes do not have stringent-enough standards?

Mr. KORNZE. Mr. Chairman, good to see you. I had the chance to be in your great state a few weeks ago. Look forward to going back.

Our rule—we actually had a similar discussion in the Senate when I testified on this matter. We did not take the approach to sort of give grades to the states and other regulators that are out there. What we looked at is what best management practices are. We took in 1.5 million public comments on this rule, and we had two draft versions for the world to work on with us.

So, we took a holistic view about where has industry gone, where have best practices gone, and what should a basic floor be, in terms of standards for Federal lands.

Mr. LAMBORN. OK. With that in mind, then, you are not contending that a state like Colorado, for instance, which has a very active regulatory regime, has been insufficient in its regulations. You've never made a finding like that concerning Colorado, did you?

Mr. KORNZE. No, sir.

Mr. LAMBORN. OK, thank you. Then why is it that you feel Colorado has to have an additional layer of regulation, if you haven't found them to be lacking in some way?

Mr. KORNZE. When it comes to regulated oil and gas, the BLM has, for instance, we have updated more than 40 different regulations—well, excuse me, almost 40 different regulations since the 1980s for the oil and gas program. So, not only have we been regulating a complex oil and gas regime on public lands, on tribal lands, but we have continuously been updating that system.

So, the concept that this update is any different than those before, I think, is difficult to get my arms around, in that this is a—as industry progresses, our regulation progresses, to make sure that we are matching robust development with responsible protection of the public lands.

Mr. LAMBORN. OK. Getting back to Colorado as an example, because I am most familiar with that. If they were already doing an adequate job—I mean you are not saying that they were dropping the ball in some tangible, specific way—then why were they not allowed to continue on doing their regulations, and you only stepping in to states that were not doing a good job?

Mr. KORNZE. Well, as we interact with the public on this issue, we received many, many requests—and folks like the Secretary of Energy's Advisory Board over at DOE and others, have pointed to the fact that there needs to be a serious upgrade in the regulations that the Federal Government has, when it comes to hydraulic fracturing, to address modern practices. The last time that our regulations on this issue, which I think the professor well pointed out, regulating on stimulation has stretched back to the 1940s, so there is nothing new about this.

But in terms of the last regulatory upgrade on the BLM side, that was in the 1980s, and we have seen a huge change in the industry in the late 1990s and early 2000s related to the use of hydraulic fracturing and horizontal drilling. So we are excited about the energy development that comes with that, we are excited about the additional progress for western economies. But at the same time, we need to make sure that we have the rules of the road in place to make sure it is done safely. There have been a lot of concerns on the part of the public, and so we are working to balance that situation.

Mr. LAMBORN. Now, let me point out for the record that the 1940's regulation you talked about was just a notice, a requirement of notice. It wasn't a full-blown regulation.

So, if states like Colorado were acting in the presence of a vacuum, you might say, by BLM, and you don't allege that they were doing anything wrong, why did you not allow them or responsible tribes, like the Ute Indians, why were they not allowed to continue with responsible regulations, and you only regulate those states that did not have regulations in place, or had poor regulations in place? Why didn't you give them that right?

Mr. KORNZE. Well, the way it works with states like Colorado, is Colorado looks at modern practice, and they update their regulations on a regular basis, similar to us. We update our regulations as practices change. The tribe, I understand, in the last few weeks has updated their regulations. So this is a system that is ongoing, and it is a cooperative, broad relationship that has existed and will continue to exist.

Mr. LAMBORN. OK. Now, with everyone's indulgence, I am going to ask a 30-second question of Mr. Hetrick. And I have to be leaving, I won't be able to stay until the end of the hearing for the second round, so I apologize.

But, Mr. Hetrick, what happens economically with drillers and producers when they have two layers of regulation to deal with, Federal and state, as opposed to just a responsible state like Colorado only?

Mr. HETRICK. Well, in 2014, in the state of Utah, we submitted about 250 permits under BLM jurisdiction, and we got completeness letters for 248 of them. So for all but two we were complete within 10 days, and we received their acknowledgment for it. But the approval time was from 180 to 270 days for those Federal permits, where on the state side we get the approval in weeks.

So, because of the additional lead time to get approval for these permits, we have to request additional ones to cover operational options that may happen 6 or 9 months down the road.

Mr. LAMBORN. OK, thank you very much. The Chair now recognizes Representative Cartwright.

Mr. CARTWRIGHT. Thank you, Mr. Chairman. I would like to yield for a moment to Mr. Polis of Colorado.

Mr. POLIS. I just wanted to clarify that the sentiments expressed by the Chair are far from universal in Colorado. I think the majority of Coloradans believe that we have, effectively, no regulations around fracking, because we don't. We have an outdated patchwork from the 1950s. No meaningful state safety regulations. We welcome any Federal floor. I have expressed the same to Secretary Jewell, because we are an example of a state that has, effectively, no regulations around fracking safety.

And I will yield back to the gentleman from Pennsylvania.

Mr. CARTWRIGHT. Thank you, Mr. Polis.

Mr. Chairman, every time we have a hearing on this subject, the Majority gets somebody to say that there is no proven case of fracking contaminating a water supply. That is a semantics game, since there are plenty of cases of oil and gas drilling contaminating water supplies.

EPA highlighted instances of casing or cementing failures that led to drinking water contamination in Ohio, North Dakota, and Colorado. It found that 600 wells drilled in 2009 and 2010 did not have cement covering, supposedly protecting groundwater resources, leaving them at high risk for contamination.

Now, I am from Pennsylvania. Pennsylvania groundwater contamination has been linked to leaky, failing, or improperly designed casings. And there are cementing casings or well construction violations at 3 percent of all shale gas wells.

In 2013, there were nearly 600 documented cases of wastewater and chemical spills in Pennsylvania. The EPA estimates that there are as many as 12 chemical spills for every 100 oil and gas wells in Pennsylvania, of which there are almost 8,000 currently operating gas wells in the Commonwealth. While well construction problems, leaky pits, or surface spills undeniably cause water contamination, the Majority always falls back on the fact that no one could point to a case where contamination was due to the fracking part of the process itself.

But just 2 months ago, a paper in the proceedings of the National Academy of Sciences studied a contaminated aquifer in Pennsylvania and found "the most likely explanation is that stray natural gas and drilling, or hydraulic fracturing compounds, were driven 1 to 3 kilometers along shallow to intermediate-depth fractures to the aquifer used as a potable water source."

More importantly, it doesn't matter to the family whose water is undrinkable whether that is due to fracking, a poorly built well, or a spill. It is all related to the fracking activity.

If we are going to move forward with fracking as part of the solution under the all-of-the-above energy strategy, we need to make sure that the process, the entire process, is safe, from start to finish.

Professor Wiseman, could you tell us briefly about some of the problems that you are aware of that oil and gas activities surrounding fracking, in addition to the frack itself, pose to drinking water supplies?

Ms. WISEMAN. Thank you, Congressman Cartwright. In addition to the Environmental Protection Agency incident that I mentioned previously in North Dakota, in which the incident appears to have occurred during fracturing and appears to have potentially sent chemicals into groundwater, as you mentioned, there have been multiple instances of the casing of the wells having problems with integrity.

I refer to those instances in my written testimony, several examples from the state of Pennsylvania noted by inspectors: December 2010, methane migrated to the surface through cement in the $9\frac{5}{8}$-inch annulus; Bradford County, Pennsylvania, initial complaint water well shows methane levels increased from non-detectable to 82.7 milligrams per liter; Chesapeake caused or allowed gas from lower formations to enter fresh groundwater.

You also mentioned spills. I believe there have been more incidents of spills noted than of well integrity problems, spills of flowback fluid, as well as hydraulic fracturing chemicals. In 2013, one paper estimates approximately 439 flowback spills in Pennsylvania. Those are several examples from the literature.

Mr. CARTWRIGHT. Well, thank you, Professor. I think this really emphasizes the need to have and enforce strong regulations at all levels. When you are dealing with public health and safety, you shouldn't have to wait for the Deepwater Horizon-like disaster to happen before implementing prudent precautionary regulations.

We don't have a widespread systemic problem with plane crashes in this country, but we have strong aviation regulations designed to prevent that and protect public safety. I think drinking water is just as important. I yield back.

Mr. BISHOP [presiding]. Thank you.

Mr. Gohmert.

Mr. GOHMERT. Thank you, Mr. Chairman. I think we have highlighted what are the problems that most Americans have with the Federal Government. Comments along the lines that it doesn't matter whether pollution is the result of fracking or casing or whatever; if it is polluted, it doesn't matter. See, that is a problem. Because for some of us who care deeply about the poorest in our country that cannot afford to pay their energy bills, and cannot afford to have a government over-reach and put regulations that raises the cost, that make them decide between gasoline and food, it does matter.

And I thought when we got an EPA study back that said—and this was a multi-year, exhaustive study, and it was one that Secretary Salazar, sitting where you guys are, actually was commenting on in this room. I kept asking him, "Is there any study that directly shows that hydraulic fracturing has polluted groundwater," and he kept beating around the bush several times. Finally he had to say, "No, there is not, but the EPA is doing an exhaustive study and we don't have that back yet."

Well, we got it back. And it says that fracking has had no widespread systemic impacts on drinking water resources in the United States.

Mr. Kornze, your testimony claims the rule "establishes requirements designed to prevent problems with complex hydraulic fracturing regulations." Well, there is no problem that existed.

Secretary Salazar said, "We haven't found one yet, but hold on, the EPA is out there studying, and they will tell us. We think they will find something." Well, they didn't. Yet you come in with your regulations that are going to raise the cost of gasoline, of all kinds of things that the poorest in this Nation need just to get by, and you don't care, because it doesn't matter to you whether the pollution comes from fracking or casing or some other problem. Well, it matters to the poorest in this country, whether they are going to be able to buy food or gasoline.

I know, apparently, it doesn't matter to you. So you come in here with these kinds of robust regulations, and you really are a solution in search of a problem, because the problem has been found not to exist with fracking. I would think that most Americans would say, "Wow, this fracking that is allowing us, if we will pursue it, to be energy independent, is a gift for those who believe in nature's God. Wow, nature's God has given us a gift," probably the only country in the world that has all the different energy and minerals that we have. And then you come in, in search of a problem with your solution. And it is outrageous.

When we look at the production from Federal lands and how it has dramatically dropped compared to the energy being produced from private lands, it is staggering what you have done.

Did you not care that the EPA found there was no groundwater problems with fracking, Mr. Kornze?

Mr. KORNZE. Well, sir, I appreciate the opportunity to answer.

Mr. GOHMERT. Oh, I bet you do.

[Laughter.]

Mr. KORNZE. Our goal is to make sure that we have robust energy development on public lands, and it is done safely.

Mr. GOHMERT. Wow. Then I wish you would have robust concerns about not having energy development, and maybe it would start going up instead of going down. Your concerns are about to destroy energy on public lands.

Let me ask you, though. Isn't it true that the states control use of water—this is the old adage—and the Federal Government is supposed to control the quality of water? Isn't that right?

Mr. KORNZE. Well, sir, on the——

Mr. GOHMERT. Do you agree with that old adage?

Mr. KORNZE. On the production point, I think it is important to point out that during this Administration, oil production on public lands has gone up by roughly—on public and tribal lands, which you need a BLM permit for both—about 80 percent. So we have gone up dramatically, so——

Mr. GOHMERT. Well, you are going to have to show me those numbers, because the numbers I have officially show that we are down. Let's see, the total Federal production percentage of U.S. total was at 36.4 percent in 2010. After your robust regulation, now it is down to 21.4. Quit helping the energy industry and it will do a lot better. I yield back.

Mr. BISHOP. Thank you. Mr. Grijalva, you are too far away down there for me to say sarcastic things to you. I am just going to have to do it by telepathy. But you are also recognized for 5 minutes.

Mr. GRIJALVA. And with that telepathy, thank you, Mr. Chairman. You started way early.

[Laughter.]

Mr. GRIJALVA. I have been catching them for a while.

Mr. Kornze, just a couple of questions. Yes or no, do you really care about poor people?

[Laughter.]

Mr. GRIJALVA. My question is the poorest in our Nation are also very concerned about the health and safety of themselves and their families.

Mr. KORNZE. Yes.

Mr. GRIJALVA. And, as a Member here that felt you didn't go far enough in the rule, the fact remains that you set a floor here. And, in that floor, my question is—you hear constantly that industry, left to its own devices, will take care of everything and go forward, and they will expedite, they will be able to get more out, faster, lower cost, the consumer will benefit, and there will be no environmental problems, there will be no health and safety problems. It will never be anything that happens that we would consider to be a hazard to the health and safety of the American people.

Now, the states say, "We do a much better job." Do you believe the states have demonstrated that there is no need for any Federal rule here, or are there ways that this rule can actually help states improve what they are doing, in terms of how they are regulating?

And, in terms of industry, should they be the only ones to be the sole arbitrators of what gets done and what doesn't get done, in terms of regulation? In other words, have none?

Mr. KORNZE. OK. Well, thank you, Ranking Member. So I think two points on that.

One is that this body has given us responsibility to have oversight responsibility for oil and gas development on public and tribal lands. That is established in law. So, we are working on that, we are proud to carry that obligation, which has been given to us by Congress.

Related to making sure that this is done appropriately, I think the EPA study has pointed out for us that there are many things that we can all be doing better. So, I think as more information comes forward, there is a lot for us to learn, and there has been a major transformation in the extractive approach to oil and gas in recent years, and we need to adjust with it to make sure that we can continue in that direction, and that we are making sure it is done safely and responsibly.

Mr. GRIJALVA. Thank you. One last question, Mr. Chairman.

Mr. Councilman, as the whole question of trust responsibility and sovereignty for native nations evolves in this country, both in law and in practice, the issue of sovereign governments, native nations being able to have both regulatory control over their resources and both—control over the resources, including this instance, regulation, I fundamentally don't have a problem with that concept, because I believe in it. I think sometimes Congress uses it situationally. In one area, and this one, sovereignty is good. In other areas, the issue of sovereignty becomes problematic to people, whether it is the protection of a sacred site and other things, that becomes a problem. In this instance, it is OK, and we agree on that.

My question to you, as a representative of tribal government and your people, is that when the self-determination comes into a regulatory scheme, and you are regulating the fracking that is occurring on your own land, as a sovereign decision, do you see right now what the government is doing as an intrusion? I understand that. But, in terms of standards and levels of regulation for health and safety for your members, how do you see that as an exercise of sovereignty, in terms of what regulations you put down?

Mr. OLGUIN. As a person sitting on tribal council, it is our sworn duty to protect our people, protect our land, and our resources. And with that, we do exercise sovereignty on a daily basis, just in the decisions we make. We have to ensure that we do that in a manner that is in perpetuity, as well.

Mr. GRIJALVA. Got it.

Mr. OLGUIN. We have to exercise these rights that were given to us, and we maintain those rights. It is a constant battle, dealing with whatever issue it is, because we as a governing body, we decide for our own people, and we emphasize that.

Mr. GRIJALVA. You are self-determined—the regulatory scheme that you would use on tribal land, that would be transparent, public, members would know about it. It would be something that the council would, in their exercise of their role, make available to all the members——

Mr. OLGUIN. Yes, we make all our rules and all our laws——

Mr. GRIJALVA. Yield back, thank you.

Mrs. LUMMIS [presiding]. The Chair now recognizes herself for 5 minutes. I want to start by saying, I am not an apologist for the oil and gas industry. I was raised next to a refinery, right next to a refinery. And I am glad that RCRA exists, because that law was necessary for us to enforce or stop the migration of hydrocarbons from that refinery onto our adjacent private land. And I am glad that regulations exist so surface owners who don't own their mineral rights can protect their surface estates, because I am in that situation, and had a bad experience with an oil company who signed a surface agreement and then violated it and damaged our surface.

So, believe me, I am not an apologist for the oil and gas industry. But I am an advocate for my state. And the state of Wyoming has done a wonderful job creating a national model for fracking regulations.

I am sorry that Tom Fitzsimmons, who is a Commissioner on the Wyoming Oil and Gas Conservation Commission, couldn't be here today. His plane was canceled, due to weather. But I used to be on the Oil and Gas Conservation Commission in Wyoming, so I will do my best to fill in.

Mr. Kornze, the Wyoming Oil and Gas Conservation Commission, which has rules and regulations that Secretary Jewell and you have applauded and held up as good examples of fracking regulations, they sent you a letter on May 29, 2015. They had requested a variance from the Federal BLM rules, because of Wyoming's superior regime for regulating fracking. They haven't heard from you. When do you intend to respond to that letter?

Mr. KORNZE. So, Chairwoman, good to see you. Related to that specific letter, I mentioned in the opening that one of the things that has happened as a result of the postponement of the effective date of the rule is that we have had to put a pause on some activities like that one, related to giving any sort of official endorsement that would be part of carrying out the regulation.

Mrs. LUMMIS. Well, let me point out that this May 29 letter to you includes a statement by the Wyoming Oil and Gas Conservation Commission Supervisor, and I quote, "There have already been several cases of Federal minerals being excluded from drilling and spacing units, due to the length of time it takes BLM to approve an application for a permit to drill."

When you have an oil and gas unit, and they drill down, and then they drill horizontally, they are drilling under fee land, under state land, under Federal land. And they are also fracking under those lands. If there is no opportunity for the state of Wyoming to regulate that fracking, which covers multiple landowners, it causes serious problems.

Now, considering the fact that Wyoming has a superior regulatory regime, can we expect you to give Wyoming a wholesale variance, so it can continue to regulate fracking in my state?

Mr. KORNZE. We look forward to continuing—when the postponement is lifted, when the stay is lifted, we look forward to continuing those conversations. Beyond that, today I am limited with what I can say on that matter.

Mrs. LUMMIS. Let me ask, Mr. Kornze, are you engaged in discussions with other states about potential variances?

Mr. KORNZE. I would say there are background conversations taking place in some places. But in terms of formalizing any of those understandings, we are not in a position where we can formalize anything.

Mrs. LUMMIS. Are some of those states that you are having background conversations with states that are involved in the pending litigation over the rule?

Mr. KORNZE. Well, there has been some discourse between your state and the Bureau of Land Management.

Mrs. LUMMIS. What about other states that are involved in pending litigation over the rule?

Mr. KORNZE. I would have to check with my team.

Mrs. LUMMIS. What about states that aren't involved in the litigation?

Mr. KORNZE. Again, if you wanted specifics, I would have to go back and visit with my team.

Mrs. LUMMIS. Can you provide me with that information?

Mr. KORNZE. What is it, specifically, that you are looking for?

Mrs. LUMMIS. I am interested in knowing whether you are in discussions with states, other states, states other than Wyoming, during the pending litigation over the rule. I am interested in knowing whether you are talking to both non-litigants and litigant states about variances regarding the rule.

Mr. KORNZE. We can certainly check into that and follow up with you.

Mrs. LUMMIS. Thank you kindly. And I would like to enter for the record this copy of the May 29 letter from the Wyoming Oil and Gas Commission to the Acting State Director of the Wyoming BLM.

[No response.]

Mrs. LUMMIS. Without objection, so ordered.

I will now recognize the gentleman from Michigan, Mr. Benishek.

Dr. BENISHEK. Thank you, Madam Chair.

Well, thanks for being here this morning. I just have a few questions.

Mr. Kornze, did the BLM give any consideration to the economic impact that would result from imposing these regulations?

Mr. KORNZE. Yes, we do have a regulatory impact analysis, which is designed to do exactly that.

Dr. BENISHEK. So what was the impact?

Mr. KORNZE. In terms of the cost of fulfilling the regulation, the average came out to, per average operation, about—well, let me first put this in context. You know, each well that a major operator drills is usually going to cost between $5 million and $10 million.

We came out that the average cost of implementation of this rule would be an additional about $11,000. So less than one-quarter of 1 percent of even the low estimate of the drilling cost.

Dr. BENISHEK. Mr. Hetrick, do you agree with that?

Mr. HETRICK. No, sir, I don't. No, sir. That wouldn't apply to my company, the amount of additional time on the front end to prepare the application would easily surpass that.

There are operational uncertainties that have a much greater dollar value, anywhere from a few hours of operational downtime, which could be tens of thousands of dollars an hour, all the way up to the cost of a well that we drilled but were not allowed to complete, using hydraulic fracturing, because we couldn't provide either the cementing assurances, the records for the cementing assurances, or we had a disagreement on a cement evaluation log, the CEL, that our interpretation of the results of the log differed from theirs——

Dr. BENISHEK. Let me ask you this, then, Mr. Hetrick. Did you or others that you may know of have any input to this economic analysis by the BLM?

Mr. HETRICK. We had lots of opportunities to discuss this with Mr. Kornze and others. They were very generous with allowing us access to the fundamentals of the rule, the mechanics of the rule.

I did not engage on the economics, this was a part that we submitted comments through trade associations and individually, but I don't recall specifically providing any information on the economics.

Dr. BENISHEK. Mr. Kornze, can you give me the names of those people that told you that it cost $10,000 a well, and only less than 1 percent? Could you provide me with that information?

Mr. KORNZE. Well, the——

Dr. BENISHEK. No, I am asking you to get me the names of——

Mr. KORNZE. I can tell you the key person is our Assistant Secretary that signs the regulation and all the company documents. That is——

Dr. BENISHEK. But I am asking you—people like Mr. Hetrick here must have given you some input on this economic analysis that you have done, right? I am asking for the names of those people that gave you the information that it cost less than 1 percent of the cost of a well to do this. Can you provide me with that information?

Mr. KORNZE. We will be happy to provide you with our analysis that lays all that out.

Dr. BENISHEK. All right. Thank you very much.

Mr. Olguin, I understand you are the Council Member for the Southern Ute Tribe. Could you maybe elaborate a bit about the BLM's imposition of regulations, and how you feel that has imposed on your tribe's sovereignty, if at all, or—tell me a little more about that, because I missed some of the testimony.

Mr. OLGUIN. The regulations itself, which is why we had to develop our own, definitely creates delays in respect to the pre-approval process. And those delays—it creates uncertainty for producers. When we are looking at that, we want to ensure certainty so that people are actually producing oil and gas on our reservation, and certainty is a key component, when it comes to budgeting for these wells.

And, depending on the BLM through the rules, there is no guarantee that a decision would be made in a timely manner. That is the reason that we went in with our regulations, to state that we will have a 48-hour notification, which in essence, they tell us what they are going to do, they do it, and then we get their final reports, which is one of the big differences. We are providing that certainty to them, as far as the operator.

Of course, the cementing, as well, where we are requiring the cementing to be from the different casings to the surface, to get rid of this component of the usable water, as far as zoning those out.

Dr. BENISHEK. Right. Thank you.

Mr. Hetrick, one more question, while I have the time. Can you tell me about the impact this regulation has had on local and state government revenues from energy producers? Do you have any comment on that?

Mr. HETRICK. I have been given information. I provide it in my written testimony. I would just have to read it from my written testimony, but I am aware of the state of Utah a year ago had some 26 rigs running, and now has 6 or 7. Certainly the revenues, the royalties, all of the economies that flow from that have stopped. So it is not a good impact.

But I am not implying this is the result of the BLM rule. It is the global commodity price collapse. But where the BLM rule is coming in, it is making it more difficult, when prices do come up, to re-enter those low-margin basins because of the uncertainty. So we are not blaming BLM for the collapse, but the re-entry will be more difficult.

Dr. BENISHEK. Thank you. My time is up.

Mr. BISHOP. Thank you. This committee will end shortly here, so you can be grateful. You also realize we are two chairman changes away from actually setting a record.

[Laughter.]

Mr. BISHOP. That is just not going to work here, I apologize for that. I still have two more to go here.

I appreciate all of you being here. I know, Director Kornze, that you would rather be elsewhere than here at this hearing, to which I would simply say, "Quit making dippy rules, and you won't have to show up here at all, it is no problem."

I do have a couple of questions for you, if I could. In your prepared statement, you quoted that the BLM's overall intent for coordinated efforts with the state is to minimize duplication and maximize efficiency. And you also said that some activities have been—implementation of the rules have been temporarily paused as a result of litigation.

Let's assume we can go back in time. It is June 23, before the judge has put on that stay for the rule. I know Colorado was still waiting for their variances. And, as I understand, no other state actually had variances in place on June 23, did they?

Mr. KORNZE. No. You are correct, sir.

Mr. BISHOP. OK. I understand from other testimony—North Dakota also said they needed 14 new hires to be able to successfully implement the law. They were not actually implemented or hired, were they?

Mr. KORNZE. Our rule identifies that we would need about 14 additional FTEs.

Mr. BISHOP. Yes. They weren't there, though.

Mr. KORNZE. Well, we have a flexible system, and we move where we need to, like when we have to push additional bodies to high-volume offices.

Mr. BISHOP. The bottom line is still they weren't there.

Mr. KORNZE. [No response.]

Mr. BISHOP. OK. And——

Mr. KORNZE. We certainly need more support for our oil and gas program.

Mr. BISHOP. You certainly do. And instructional memoranda sent to state offices advising them of implementation rules, that did not exist on June 23, either, did it?

Mr. KORNZE. We have the rule itself, which is——

Mr. BISHOP. You didn't have the instructional memoranda with it, did you?

Mr. KORNZE. There were no——

Mr. BISHOP. OK.

Mr. KORNZE. No.

Mr. BISHOP. So, at the time just before its implementation, there were no variances that were out there, the number of people were inadequate. There was no clear guidance to the districts. And some states, like my state, which I think had been doing an excellent job in ensuring protection of the environment with hydraulic fracturing, basically felt insulted by that concept.

Now, before this rule was actually proposed, prior to that, the states were regulating hydraulic fracturing on Federal lands, right?

Mr. KORNZE. As was BLM.

Mr. BISHOP. The law says the Federal agencies cannot delegate regulatory authority to states without a specific statutory approval. What do you claim is that specific statutory approval?

Mr. KORNZE. Could you restate the question?

Mr. BISHOP. You can't delegate regulatory authority. You can be involved in the process, but you can't delegate regulatory authority, without specific approval to do so. What do you claim is the specific statutory authority allowing BLM to delegate regulatory authority to states?

Mr. KORNZE. I am not sure I fully grasp the question, but our authorities are found in FLPMA and in the Mineral Leasing Act and in the Indian mineral leasing statutes.

Mr. BISHOP. Yes, and none of that does the delegation of regulatory authority, which I understand, because that authority simply does not exist. And there are some reasons why the states have been doing it, and it could relate to states' ownership of the groundwater, that has been proposed here before.

But in any event, either the states have the right to regulate hydraulic fracturing before this rule, or because this rule does not give them that legal change. So either they have the right to regulate them before this rule, or BLM simply was negligent for decades in not doing its job in regulating the fracking by itself.

Mr. KORNZE. The BLM has had hydraulic fracturing regulations since the 1980s.

Mr. BISHOP. Regulatory regulations?

Mr. KORNZE. Yes.

Mr. BISHOP. And from which of those specific catalog of bills that you told me earlier gave you that right of regulatory fracking authority?

Mr. KORNZE. We can give you the reference after the hearing, but——

Mr. BISHOP. All right. I will look for that, too. Let me use my last minute of this hearing, actually, just to go and to follow up. I appreciate you meeting with me the other day. I asked you some questions about some of the correspondence we had. I want you to know it is my goal to try and work with the Department of the Interior to make sure that we can minimize the requests that we have. But, in addition, I've got to get something back.

So I told you about the references. I didn't tell you the specifics. It was between DOI and the Border Patrol—their correspondence since January of 2014. You all sent us 3,600 pages. Included in that was an ecological study going back to the Bicentennial. You sent us another one about how astronauts were trained in the Southwest between 1963 and 1972. You gave us a copy of a wilderness study EA from 1983 that came from the University of Minnesota library. You also gave me—the only one that actually did fit that time frame was celebratory, about regarding a party that was going to be established after the Oregon National Monument was identified.

I am sorry, that stuff didn't get to us. I ask you if you would actually do that. It seems to us as if we are almost being inundated with things that are in-your-face saying, "Screw you, we are not going to give you the material that you want." If you guys will work with us in getting those materials, I want to try and work with you all, and try to limit the kind of requests that we have.

The same thing happened with the request for data from the BLM, the Rawlins field office that dealt with bonding. The question was, "Were those bond instruments always in BLM's possession, or were they replaced?" The data that we got back from you simply said you've got them now, but it didn't go back to what the actual question was, did you actually have them or not.

So, once again, I am going to ask the question. And this is not just for BLM, this goes for the entire Department. We are having a difficult time, when we request information, of getting accurate information. So I would request once again, especially from BLM. If we are going to ask you for that data, you know, I appreciate you helped astronauts in 1963, but that is not what we needed to know.

With that, I would ask if there are any other questions, but I am the only one left here.

[Laughter.]

Mr. BISHOP. Unless you want to ask a question of me, and no, you don't have the authority to do that, statutorily or not.

With that, I want to express to the four witnesses my appreciation of you coming here, spending the time with us. It is very kind. I know that the Members, as you saw from those who came in, a whole lot came in to ask questions. It was a significant issue for them. I appreciate you spending the time doing that.

And I need to say something just in ending, that you have 10 days to do something. We may have other questions for you, as you well know. And the official words are—I already thanked you for your valuable testimony—members of the committee may have additional questions for witnesses, and we will ask you to respond to these in writing. Under Committee Rule 4(h), the hearing record will be open for 10 business days for these responses.

So, if there is no further business, without objection, the committee will stand adjourned. Thank you.

[Whereupon, at 12:25 p.m., the subcommittee was adjourned.]

[ADDITIONAL MATERIALS SUBMITTED FOR THE RECORD]

PREPARED STATEMENT OF THE HON. MATT CARTWRIGHT, A REPRESENTATIVE IN CONGRESS FROM THE STATE OF PENNSYLVANIA

BLM is currently working toward implementation of a rule that would modernize horribly outdated oil and gas regulations on Federal land. We must allow the BLM to proceed with implementing this rule to provide a national baseline to protect our environment, our water, and our Federal land from hazardous contamination.

Since the 1980s, the scale and impacts associated with the oil and gas industry have grown dramatically, but BLM's fracking regulations have not kept pace. In March 2015, the BLM finalized a modest, common-sense rule to update its 30-year-old fracking regulations. With these updates, the BLM is taking responsible steps to improve well integrity, reduce the impact of toxic wastewater, and increase transparency around chemicals used in the fracking process. Importantly, the new regulations will not impact states with robust fracking regulations and will simply set a regulatory baseline for the states without fracking regulations. Notably, in 2013, there were still 19 states with operating fracking wells that had no hydraulic fracturing regulations in place.

Presently, over 90 percent of the more than 2,500 oil and gas wells drilled each year on federally managed lands utilize hydraulic fracturing. And just this month, the EPA released a draft report that concludes that there are above and below ground mechanisms by which hazardous hydraulic fracturing chemicals have the potential to impact drinking water resources.

Because of this, the Federal Government must take the necessary steps to ensure that toxic and carcinogenic fracking chemicals do not contaminate America's water supply, streams, rivers, and lakes.

The fracking fluid injected into oil and gas wells contain thousands of chemicals, many of which can harm humans and the environment. If fact, the EPA identified over 1,000 different chemicals that have been used during hydraulic fracturing process, with an estimated 9,100 gallons of chemicals used for each well.

Due in large part to fracking loopholes and outdated oil and gas regulations, fracking chemical spills and water contaminations have occurred. In my home state of Pennsylvania, there were nearly 600 documented cases of wastewater and chemical spills in 2013 alone. In fact, the EPA estimates that there are as many as 12 chemical spills for every 100 oil and gas wells in the state of Pennsylvania.

Chemical and wastewater spills associated with fracking operations harm the environment and have been found to contaminate surface water. The EPA's draft study found that 8 percent of studied wastewater spills polluted surface or groundwater.

In addition to chemical spills, improper well construction can lead to harmful pollution. The EPA has highlighted instances of casing or cementing failures that led to drinking water contamination in Ohio, North Dakota, and Colorado. It found that 600 wells drilled in 2009 and 2010 didn't have cement covering supposedly protected groundwater resources, leaving them at high risk to contamination. In Pennsylvania, groundwater contamination has been linked to "leaky, failing, or improperly installed casings," and there are cementing, casing, or well construction violations at 3 percent of all shale gas wells.

Thankfully, the BLM's rule will help prevent fracking chemicals and wastewater from contaminating water bodies. It does so by validating the integrity of fracking wells and increasing the standards for storage and recovery of waste fluid. The rule will require companies to publicly disclose the chemicals being pumped into public lands.

I do not think that the new rule will fix all problems related to fracking. There is no reason that oil and gas development, including development which involves fracking, should be exempted from our country's landmark environmental laws. That is why I introduced the FRESHER and CLEANER Acts, which would require oil and gas development to comply with the Resources Conservation and Recovery Act and the Clean Water Act. Though legislation like this is required to further safeguard public health and safety, this rule is a good start.

I am not opposed to fracking, and I believe we must utilize our natural resources. But we must do so in a careful manner. There are bad actors in the oil and gas business that cut corners and do not drill and frack properly and safely. The states unfortunately do not all have the expertise and resources to properly manage this exploding industry. While this rule will set a relatively low bar, it is one which ensures a baseline across the country to protect our public lands, and should be implemented.

———

[LIST OF DOCUMENTS SUBMITTED FOR THE RECORD RETAINED IN THE COMMITTEE'S OFFICIAL FILES]

—May 29, 2015—Letter from the Wyoming Oil and Gas Conservation Commission to the BLM Wyoming Office requesting a variance from the regulatory provision in each of the rule's sections.

○